The UK
Tefal Digital Air Fryer
COOKBOOK
For Beginners

Easy & Delicious to Prepare Recipes for Your Tefal Digital Health Air Fryer

Scott King

Legal & Disclaimer

The information contained in this book and its contents is not designed to replace or take the place of any form of medical or professional advice; and is not meant to replace the need for independent medical, financial, legal or other professional advice or services, as may be required. The content and information in this book has been provided for educational and entertainment purposes only.

The content and information contained in this book has been compiled from sources deemed reliable, and it is accurate to the best of the Author's knowledge, information and belief. However, the Author cannot guarantee its accuracy and validity and cannot be held liable for any errors and/or omissions. Further, changes are periodically made to this book as and when needed. Where appropriate and/or necessary, you must consult a professional (including but not limited to your doctor, attorney, financial advisor or such other professional advisor) before using any of the suggested remedies, techniques, or information in this book.

Contents

SANDWICHES AND BURGERS RECIPES.................59

APPETIZERS AND SNACKS 69

VEGETARIANS RECIPES 78

VEGETABLE SIDE DISHES RECIPES.................88

INTRODUCTION

HOW DOES AN AIR FRYER WORK?

The first think you're probably wondering is how an Air Fryer works. How is it any different than a regular deep fryer or an oven? Most importantly, Air Fryers are different from regular deep fryers because they don't actually fry food, meaning you don't actually submerge your food in hot oil to cook it.

The actual mechanism of Air Fryers is most akin to that of a convection oven. Basically, your food is placed in a perforated metal basket. At the top is a heating unit with a high powered fan that blows the hot air all around the food, creating a convection effect that nicely and evenly browns the outside of the food. And unlike a convection oven, Air Fryers are compact, allowing for faster and more efficient preheating and cooking times.

1) It makes delicious food !

When you bake food in regular ovens (especially not convention ovens), you are often left with uneven results, with some parts burnt and other parts undercooked. The mechanism of Air Fryers described above allows hot air to circulate all around the food, maximizing surface area-to-heat ratio and allowing for perfectly even crispiness and crunchiness. While an Air Fryer won't taste exactly like if you used a traditional deep fryer, we really love the end result of each recipe we've tried so far.

2) It is a healthier option

Love the taste of fried food but not the way it makes you feel afterwards (for instance Zoe tends to get heartburn with fried food)? Are you disappointed with the end result when you try the oven-roasted version of the same recipe? If yes to these questions, then an Air Fryer might be the solution!

You can usually get away with using little-to-no oil when cooking with an Air Fryer, which can cut calories. Furthermore, one study (Sansano et at., 2015) showed that compared to traditional frying methods, using an air fryer reduces acrylamide (a compound associated with certain types of cancer) by up to 90%.

3) It is time and energy efficient

With their compact size and efficient circulation of hot air, Air Fryers out-compete your oven. With most recipes only needing 8-20 minutes of cooking, Air Fryers reduce cooking time by up to 25% (they also only need a fraction of the time to preheat, unlike your oven), saving you both time and energy.

4) There's an air fryer for every price range

With prices as low as $40, buying an Air Fryer doesn't have to break your wallet. We are obviously more than happy with our investment in an Air Fryer. And don't worry, even the lower-priced ones still produce great results! Keep reading this Ultimate Air Fryer Guide to see the specific products we recommend.

5) They are easy to clean

With removable parts, nonstick materials, and most being dishwasher-safe, cleaning your air fryer is no hassle at all! And compared to the grease that coats your kitchen walls after deep frying foods, an Air Fryer produces no mess.

6) They are versatile and can make all kinds of recipes

See below for a sample of all of the different types of food you can make using an Air Fryer. From meat to vegetables to even pizza, we've been able to incorporate air frying into a ton of our meal preparations.

7) Many have different modes, allowing different types of cooking

Not only used for frying foods, an Air Fryer can also be used for reheating leftovers, thawing frozen food, and much, much more. Ours lets you change the settings to "air fry", "roast", "dehydrate", and "reheat". It's up to you to experiment!

8) They come in all different shapes and sizes

It's true that they take up some counter space. But there's an Air Fryer of every size to fit your needs. If you mostly cook for one or two people, you can get away with 2 to 3 quart sized Air Fryers. If you usually cook for a family of 3-5, consider 5 to 6 quart ones. But generally, air fryers between 3 to 5 quarts are versatile enough for most types and quantities of cooking.

9) They make for a great gift

What a perfect gift for the budding home chef?! I got ours for Zoe for Christmas. But whether its for a birthday, wedding registry, or any other special occasion, an Air Fryer makes for an ideal long-lasting and useful present.

10) They let you join the Air Fryer community

With niche Air Fryer blogs to Air Fryer recipe books, buying one of these lets you drastically expand your culinary repertoire and connect with a whole new community of home chefs.

HOW TO USE AN AIR FRYER

The Air Fryer's Versatility

Get ready to challenge everything you know about frying foods. Air fryers can fry your favorite foods to crispy, golden brown perfection (yes, French fries and potato chips!) using little or no oil. Not only can you make traditionally fried foods like potato chips and French fries, but it's also great for vegetables, proteins like chicken wings and drummettes, and appetizers like coquettes and feta triangles. Even desserts like brownies and blondies are perfectly baked in an air fryer.

Why It Works

Put in other terms, an air fryer is much like a convection oven but in a different outfit, cooking food at very high temperatures while simultaneously circulating dry air around the food, cooking food faster all the while making it crisp without needing to add extra fat.

What to Look for in an Air Fryer

There are a lot of different sizes and types of air fryers available now. If you're cooking for a crowd, try an the Philips XXL Air Fryer which can cook an entire chicken or six portions of fries.

If you have limited counter space, try the Philips Avance Air Fryer which uses patented technology to circulate hot air, yielding crunchy, satisfying results. and this next-generation air fryer boasts a more compact size (same capacity!) and TurboStar technology, which ensures food cooks evenly (no more worrying about pile-ups). Now you can enjoy all the fried foods you love—without the guilt.

To up an air fryer's versatility even more, You can also buy a variety of different attachments, such as a rack, grill pan, muffin pans and mesh baskets) to for entertaining. Check out our Air Fryer seasonings that we developed in-house, ranging from Buttermilk Black Pepper Seasoning for air-frying chicken to Garlic Sichuan Seasoning perfect for Chinese cooking.

Read on for a video on the air fryer in action, how-to tips and our favorite recipes, including those fries, air-fried tonkotsu, chicken wings and more.

FIVE TIPS FOR USING AN AIR FRYER

1. Shake it.

Be sure to open the air fryer and shake foods around as they "fry" in the machine's basket—smaller foods like French fries and chips can compress. For best results, rotate them every 5-10 minutes.

2. Don't overcrowd.

Give foods plenty of space so that the air can circulate effectively; that's what gives you crispy results. Our test kitchen cooks swear by the air fryer for snacks and small batches.

3. Give foods a spray.

Lightly spray foods with cooking spray or add just a bit of oil to ensure they don't stick to the basket.

4. Keep it dry.

Pat foods dry before cooking (if they are marinated, for example) to avoid splattering and excess smoke. Similarly, when cooking high-fat foods like chicken wings, make sure to empty the fat from the bottom machine periodically.

5. Master other cooking methods.

The air fryer isn't just for frying; it's great for other healthy cooking methods like baking, roasting and grilling, too. Our test kitchen also loves to use the machine for cooking salmon!

Quiche Cups

Ingredients:

- ¼ lb. all-natural ground pork sausage
- 3 eggs
- ¾ C. milk
- 20 foil muffin cups
- cooking spray
- 4 oz. sharp Cheddar cheese, grated

Servings: 10
Cooking Time: 16 Mins.

Directions:

1. Divide sausage into 3 portions and shape each into a thin patty.
2. Place patties in air fryer basket and cook 390°F for 6minutes.
3. While sausage is cooking, prepare the egg mixture. A large measuring C. or bowl with a pouring lip works best. Combine the eggs and milk and whisk until well blended. Set aside.
4. When sausage has cooked fully, remove patties from basket, drain well, and use a fork to crumble the meat into small pieces.
5. Double the foil C. into 10 sets. Remove paper liners from the top muffin C. and spray the foil C. lightly with cooking spray.
6. Divide crumbled sausage among the 10 muffin C. sets.
7. Top each with grated cheese, divided evenly among the cups.
8. Place 5 C. in air fryer basket.
9. Pour egg mixture into each cup, filling until each C. is at least ⅔ full.
10. Cook for 8 Mins. and test for doneness. A knife inserted into the center shouldn't have any raw egg on it when removed.
11. If needed, cook 2 more minutes, until egg completely sets.
12. Repeat steps 8 through 11 for the remaining quiches.

Pepperoni Pizza Bread

Ingredients:

- 7-inch round bread boule
- 2 C. grated mozzarella cheese
- 1 tbsp. dried oregano
- 1 C. pizza sauce
- 1 C. mini pepperoni or pepperoni slices, cut in quarters
- Pizza sauce for dipping (optional)

Servings: 4
Cooking Time:
15 Mins.

Directions:

1. Make 7 to 8 deep slices across the bread boule, leaving 1 inch of bread uncut at the bottom of every slice before you reach the cutting board. The slices should go about three quarters of the way through the boule and be about 2 inches apart from each other. Turn the bread boule 90 degrees and make 7 to 8 similar slices perpendicular to the first slices to form squares in the bread. Again, make sure you don't cut all the way through the bread.

2. Combine the mozzarella cheese and oregano in a small bowl.

3. Fill the slices in the bread with pizza sauce by gently spreading the bread apart and spooning the sauce in between the squares of bread. Top the sauce with the mozzarella cheese mixture and then the pepperoni. Do your very best to get the cheese and pepperoni in between the slices, rather than on top of the bread. Keep spreading the bread apart and stuffing the ingredients in, but be careful not to tear the bottom of the bread.

4. Preheat the air fryer to 320°F.

5. Transfer the bread boule to the air fryer basket and air-fry for 15 minutes, making sure the top doesn't get too dark. (It will just be the cheese on top that gets dark, so if you've done a good job of tucking the cheese in between the slices, this shouldn't be an issue.)

6. Carefully remove the bread from the basket with a spatula. Transfer it to a serving platter with more sauce to dip into if desired. Serve with a lot of napkins so that people can just pull the bread apart with their hands and enjoy!

Strawberry Toast

Ingredients:

- 4 slices bread, ½-inch thick
- butter-flavored cooking spray
- 1 C. sliced strawberries
- 1 tsp. sugar

Servings: 4
Cooking Time:
8 Mins.

Directions:

1. Spray one side of each bread slice with butter-flavored cooking spray. Lay slices sprayed side down.
2. Divide the strawberries among the bread slices.
3. Sprinkle evenly with the sugar and place in the air fryer basket in a single layer.
4. Cook at 390°F for 8minutes. The bottom should look brown and crisp and the top should look glazed.

Orange Rolls

Ingredients:

- parchment paper
- 3 oz. low-fat cream cheese
- 1 tbsp. low-fat sour cream or plain yogurt (not Greek yogurt)
- 2 tsp. sugar
- ¼ tsp. pure vanilla extract
- ¼ tsp. orange extract
- 1 can (8 count) organic crescent roll dough
- ¼ C. chopped walnuts
- ¼ C. dried cranberries
- ¼ C. shredded, sweetened coconut
- butter-flavored cooking spray
- Orange Glaze
- ½ C. powdered sugar
- 1 tbsp. orange juice
- ¼ tsp. orange extract
- dash of salt

Directions:

1. Cut a circular piece of parchment paper slightly smaller than the bottom of your air fryer basket. Set aside.
2. In a small bowl, combine the cream cheese, sour cream or yogurt, sugar, and vanilla and orange extracts. Stir until smooth.
3. Preheat air fryer to 300°F.
4. Separate crescent roll dough into 8 triangles and divide cream cheese mixture among them. Starting at wide end, spread cheese mixture to within 1 inch of point.
5. Sprinkle nuts and cranberries evenly over cheese mixture.
6. Starting at wide end, roll up triangles, then sprinkle with coconut, pressing in lightly to make it stick. Spray tops of rolls with butter-flavored cooking spray.
7. Place parchment paper in air fryer basket, and place 4 rolls on top, spaced evenly.
8. Cook for 10minutes, until rolls are golden brown and cooked through.
9. Repeat steps 7 and 8 to cook remaining 4 rolls. You should be able to use the same piece of parchment paper twice.
10. In a small bowl, stir together ingredients for glaze and drizzle over warm rolls.

Sweet-hot Pepperoni Pizza

Ingredients:

- 1 (6- to 8-ounce) pizza dough ball*
- olive oil
- ½ C. pizza sauce
- ¾ C. grated mozzarella cheese
- ½ C. thick sliced pepperoni
- ⅓ C. sliced pickled hot banana peppers
- ¼ tsp. dried oregano
- 2 tsp. honey

Servings: 2
Cooking Time:
18 Mins.

Directions:

1. Preheat the air fryer to 390°F.
2. Cut out a piece of aluminum foil the same size as the bottom of the air fryer basket. Brush the foil circle with olive oil. Shape the dough into a circle and place it on top of the foil. Dock the dough by piercing it several times with a fork. Brush the dough lightly with olive oil and transfer it into the air fryer basket with the foil on the bottom.
3. Air-fry the plain pizza dough for 6 minutes. Turn the dough over, remove the aluminum foil and brush again with olive oil. Air-fry for an additional 4 minutes.
4. Spread the pizza sauce on top of the dough and sprinkle the mozzarella cheese over the sauce. Top with the pepperoni, pepper slices and dried oregano. Lower the temperature of the air fryer to 350°F and cook for 8 minutes, until the cheese has melted and lightly browned. Transfer the pizza to a cutting board and drizzle with the honey. Slice and serve.

Pumpkin Loaf

Ingredients:

- cooking spray
- 1 large egg
- ½ C. granulated sugar
- ⅓ C. oil
- ½ C. canned pumpkin (not pie filling)
- ½ tsp. vanilla
- ⅔ C. flour plus 1 tablespoon
- ½ tsp. baking powder
- ½ tsp. baking soda
- ½ tsp. salt
- 1 tsp. pumpkin pie spice
- ¼ tsp. cinnamon

Directions:

1. Spray 6 x 6-inch baking dish lightly with cooking spray.
2. Place baking dish in air fryer basket and preheat air fryer to 330°F.
3. In a large bowl, beat eggs and sugar together with a hand mixer.
4. Add oil, pumpkin, and vanilla and mix well.
5. Sift together all dry ingredients. Add to pumpkin mixture and beat well, about 1 minute.
6. Pour batter in baking dish and cook at 330°F for 22 Mins. or until toothpick inserted in center of loaf comes out clean.

Chocolate Chip Banana Muffins

Ingredients:

Servings: 12
Cooking Time: 14 Mins.

- 2 medium bananas, mashed
- ¼ C. brown sugar
- 1½ tsp. vanilla extract
- ⅔ C. milk
- 2 tbsp. butter
- 1 large egg
- 1 C. white whole-wheat flour
- ½ C. old-fashioned oats
- 1 tsp. baking soda
- ½ tsp. baking powder
- ⅛ tsp. sea salt
- ¼ C. mini chocolate chips

Directions:

1. Preheat the air fryer to 330°F.
2. In a large bowl, combine the bananas, brown sugar, vanilla extract, milk, butter, and egg; set aside.
3. In a separate bowl, combine the flour, oats, baking soda, baking powder, and salt.
4. Slowly add the dry ingredients into the wet ingredients, folding in the flour mixture ⅓ C. at a time.
5. Mix in the chocolate chips and set aside.
6. Using silicone muffin liners, fill 6 muffin liners two-thirds full. Carefully place the muffin liners in the air fryer basket and bake for 20 Mins. (or until the tops are browned and a toothpick inserted in the center comes out clean). Carefully remove the muffins from the basket and repeat with the remaining batter.
7. Serve warm.

Oat Bran Muffins

Ingredients:

- ⅔ C. oat bran
- ½ C. flour
- ¼ C. brown sugar
- 1 tsp. baking powder
- ½ tsp. baking soda
- ⅛ tsp. salt
- ½ C. buttermilk
- 1 egg
- 2 tbsp. canola oil
- ½ C. chopped dates, raisins, or dried cranberries
- 24 paper muffin cups
- cooking spray

Servings: 8
Cooking Time:
12 Mins.

Directions:

1. Preheat air fryer to 330°F.
2. In a large bowl, combine the oat bran, flour, brown sugar, baking powder, baking soda, and salt.
3. In a small bowl, beat together the buttermilk, egg, and oil.
4. Pour buttermilk mixture into bowl with dry ingredients and stir just until moistened. Do not beat.
5. Gently stir in dried fruit.
6. Use triple baking C. to help muffins hold shape during baking. Spray them with cooking spray, place 4 sets of C. in air fryer basket at a time, and fill each one ¾ full of batter.
7. Cook for 12minutes, until top springs back when lightly touched and toothpick inserted in center comes out clean.
8. Repeat for remaining muffins.

Cheddar Cheese Biscuits

Ingredients:

- 2⅓ C. self-rising flour
- 2 tbsp. sugar
- ½ C. butter (1 stick), frozen for 15 Mins.
- ½ C. grated Cheddar cheese, plus more to melt on top
- 1⅓ C. buttermilk
- 1 C. all-purpose flour, for shaping
- 1 tbsp. butter, melted

Servings: 8
Cooking Time:
22 Mins.

Directions:

1. Line a buttered 7-inch metal cake pan with parchment paper or a silicone liner.

2. Combine the flour and sugar in a large mixing bowl. Grate the butter into the flour. Add the grated cheese and stir to coat the cheese and butter with flour. Then add the buttermilk and stir just until you can no longer see streaks of flour. The dough should be quite wet.

3. Spread the all-purpose (not self-rising) flour out on a small cookie sheet. With a spoon, scoop 8 evenly sized balls of dough into the flour, making sure they don't touch each other. With floured hands, coat each dough ball with flour and toss them gently from hand to hand to shake off any excess flour. Place each floured dough ball into the prepared pan, right up next to the other. This will help the biscuits rise up, rather than spreading out.

4. Preheat the air fryer to 380°F.

5. Transfer the cake pan to the basket of the air fryer, lowering it into the basket using a sling made of aluminum foil (fold a piece of aluminum foil into a strip about 2-inches wide by 24-inches long). Let the ends of the aluminum foil sling hang across the cake pan before returning the basket to the air fryer.

6. Air-fry for 20 minutes. Check the biscuits a couple of times to make sure they are not getting too brown on top. If they are, re-arrange the aluminum foil strips to cover any brown parts. After 20 minutes, check the biscuits by inserting a toothpick into the center of the biscuits. It should come out clean. If it needs a little more time, continue to air-fry for a couple of extra minutes. Brush the tops of the biscuits with some melted butter and sprinkle a little more grated cheese on top if desired. Pop the basket back into the air fryer for another 2 minutes. Remove the cake pan from the air fryer using the aluminum sling. Let the biscuits cool for just a minute or two and then turn them out onto a plate and pull apart. Serve immediately.

S'mores Pockets

Ingredients:

- 12 sheets phyllo dough, thawed
- 1½ C. butter, melted
- ¾ C. graham cracker crumbs
- 1 (7-ounce) Giant Hershey's® milk chocolate bar
- 12 marshmallows, cut in half

Servings: 6
Cooking Time:
5 Mins.

Directions:

1. Place one sheet of the phyllo on a large cutting board. Keep the rest of the phyllo sheets covered with a slightly damp, clean kitchen towel. Brush the phyllo sheet generously with some melted butter. Place a second phyllo sheet on top of the first and brush it with more butter. Repeat with one more phyllo sheet until you have a stack of 3 phyllo sheets with butter brushed between the layers. Cover the phyllo sheets with one quarter of the graham cracker crumbs leaving a 1-inch border on one of the short ends of the rectangle. Cut the phyllo sheets lengthwise into 3 strips.

2. Take 2 of the strips and crisscross them to form a cross with the empty borders at the top and to the left. Place 2 of the chocolate rectangles in the center of the cross. Place 4 of the marshmallow halves on top of the chocolate. Now fold the pocket together by folding the bottom phyllo strip up over the chocolate and marshmallows. Then fold the right side over, then the top strip down and finally the left side over. Brush all the edges generously with melted butter to seal shut. Repeat with the next three sheets of phyllo, until all the sheets have been used. You will be able to make 2 pockets with every second batch because you will have an extra graham cracker crumb strip from the previous set of sheets.

3. Preheat the air fryer to 350°F.

4. Transfer 3 pockets at a time to the air fryer basket. Air-fry at 350°F for 4 to 5 minutes, until the phyllo dough is light brown in color. Flip the pockets over halfway through the cooking process. Repeat with the remaining 3 pockets.

5. Serve warm.

Fried Twinkies

Ingredients:

- 2 Large egg white(s)
- 2 tbsp. Water
- 1½ C. (about 9 ounces) Ground gingersnap cookie crumbs
- 6 Twinkies
- Vegetable oil spray

Directions:

1. Preheat the air fryer to 400°F.

2. Set up and fill two shallow soup plates or small pie plates on your counter: one for the egg white(s), whisked with the water until foamy; and one for the gingersnap crumbs.

3. Dip a Twinkie in the egg white(s), turning it to coat on all sides, even the ends. Let the excess egg white mixture slip back into the rest, then set the Twinkie in the crumbs. Roll it to coat on all sides, even the ends, pressing gently to get an even coating. Then repeat this process: egg white(s), followed by crumbs. Lightly coat the prepared Twinkie on all sides with vegetable oil spray. Set aside and coat each of the remaining Twinkies with the same double-dipping technique, followed by spraying.

4. Set the Twinkies flat side up in the basket with as much air space between them as possible. Air-fry for 5 minutes, or until browned and crunchy.

5. Use a nonstick-safe spatula to gently transfer the Twinkies to a wire rack. Cool for at least 10 Mins. before serving.

Cheese Blintzes

Ingredients:

- 1½ 7½-ounce package(s) farmer cheese
- 3 tbsp. Regular or low-fat cream cheese (not fat-free)
- 3 tbsp. Granulated white sugar
- ¼ tsp. Vanilla extract
- 6 Egg roll wrappers
- 3 tbsp. Butter, melted and cooled

Servings: 6
Cooking Time:
10 Mins.

Directions:

1. Preheat the air fryer to 375°F .
2. Use a flatware fork to mash the farmer cheese, cream cheese, sugar, and vanilla in a small bowl until smooth.
3. Set one egg roll wrapper on a clean, dry work surface. Place ¼ C. of the filling at the edge closest to you, leaving a ½-inch gap before the edge of the wrapper. Dip your clean finger in water and wet the edges of the wrapper. Fold the perpendicular sides over the filling, then roll the wrapper closed with the filling inside. Set it aside seam side down and continue filling the remainder of the wrappers.
4. Brush the wrappers on all sides with the melted butter. Be generous. Set them seam side down in the basket with as much space between them as possible. Air-fry undisturbed for 10 minutes, or until lightly browned.
5. Use a nonstick-safe spatula to transfer the blintzes to a wire rack. Cool for at least 5 Mins. or up to 20 Mins. before serving.

Pear And Almond Biscotti Crumble

Ingredients:

- 7-inch cake pan or ceramic dish
- 3 pears, peeled, cored and sliced
- ½ C. brown sugar
- ¼ tsp. ground ginger
- 1 tsp. ground cinnamon
- ⅛ tsp. ground nutmeg
- 2 tbsp. cornstarch
- 1¼ C. (4 to 5) almond biscotti, coarsely crushed
- ¼ C. all-purpose flour
- ¼ C. sliced almonds
- ¼ C. butter, melted

Directions:

1. Combine the pears, brown sugar, ginger, cinnamon, nutmeg and cornstarch in a bowl. Toss to combine and then pour the pear mixture into a greased 7-inch cake pan or ceramic dish.
2. Combine the crushed biscotti, flour, almonds and melted butter in a medium bowl. Toss with a fork until the mixture resembles large crumbles. Sprinkle the biscotti crumble over the pears and cover the pan with aluminum foil.
3. Preheat the air fryer to 350°F.
4. Air-fry at 350°F for 60 minutes. Remove the aluminum foil and air-fry for an additional 5 Mins. to brown the crumble layer.
5. Serve warm.

Baked Apple

Ingredients:

- 3 small Honey Crisp or other baking apples
- 3 tbsp. maple syrup
- 3 tbsp. chopped pecans
- 1 tbsp. firm butter, cut into 6 pieces

Servings: 6
Cooking Time:
20 Mins.

Directions:

1. Put ½ C. water in the drawer of the air fryer.
2. Wash apples well and dry them.
3. Split apples in half. Remove core and a little of the flesh to make a cavity for the pecans.
4. Place apple halves in air fryer basket, cut side up.
5. Spoon 1½ tsp. pecans into each cavity.
6. Spoon ½ tbsp. maple syrup over pecans in each apple.
7. Top each apple with ½ tsp. butter.
8. Cook at 360°F for 20 minutes, until apples are tender.

Black And Blue Clafoutis

Ingredients:

- 6-inch pie pan
- 3 large eggs
- ½ C. sugar
- 1 tsp. vanilla extract
- 2 tbsp. butter, melted 1 C. milk
- ½ C. all-purpose flour*
- 1 C. blackberries
- 1 C. blueberries
- 2 tbsp. confectioners' sugar

Directions:

1. Preheat the air fryer to 320°F.
2. Combine the eggs and sugar in a bowl and whisk vigorously until smooth, lighter in color and well combined. Add the vanilla extract, butter and milk and whisk together well. Add the flour and whisk just until no lumps or streaks of white remain.
3. Scatter half the blueberries and blackberries in a greased (6-inch) pie pan or cake pan. Pour half of the batter (about 1¼ cups) on top of the berries and transfer the tart pan to the air fryer basket. You can use an aluminum foil sling to help with this by taking a long piece of aluminum foil, folding it in half lengthwise twice until it is roughly 26-inches by 3-inches. Place this under the pie dish and hold the ends of the foil to move the pie dish in and out of the air fryer basket. Tuck the ends of the foil beside the pie dish while it cooks in the air fryer.
4. Air-fry at 320°F for 15 Mins. or until the clafoutis has puffed up and is still a little jiggly in the center. Remove the clafoutis from the air fryer, invert it onto a plate and let it cool while you bake the second batch. Serve the clafoutis warm, dusted with confectioners' sugar on top.

Fried Snickers Bars

Ingredients:

- ⅓ C. All-purpose flour
- 1 Large egg white(s), beaten until foamy
- 1½ C. (6 ounces) Vanilla wafer cookie crumbs
- 8 Fun-size (0.6-ounce/17-gram) Snickers bars, frozen
- Vegetable oil spray

Servings: 8
Cooking Time:
4 Mins.

Directions:

1. Preheat the air fryer to 400°F.

2. Set up and fill three shallow soup plates or small pie plates on your counter: one for the flour, one for the beaten egg white(s), and one for the cookie crumbs.

3. Unwrap the frozen candy bars. Dip one in the flour, turning it to coat on all sides. Gently shake off any excess, then set it in the beaten egg white(s). Turn it to coat all sides, even the ends, then let any excess egg white slip back into the rest. Set the candy bar in the cookie crumbs. Turn to coat on all sides, even the ends. Dip the candy bar back in the egg white(s) a second time, then into the cookie crumbs a second time, making sure you have an even coating all around. Coat the covered candy bar all over with vegetable oil spray. Set aside so you can dip and coat the remaining candy bars.

4. Set the coated candy bars in the basket with as much air space between them as possible. Air-fry undisturbed for 4 minutes, or until golden brown.

5. Remove the basket from the machine and let the candy bars cool in the basket for 10 minutes. Use a nonstick-safe spatula to transfer them to a wire rack and cool for 5 Mins. more before chowing down.

Honey-roasted Mixed Nuts

Ingredients:

- ½ C. raw, shelled pistachios
- ½ C. raw almonds
- 1 C. raw walnuts
- 2 tbsp. filtered water
- 2 tbsp. honey
- 1 tbsp. vegetable oil
- 2 tbsp. sugar
- ½ tsp. salt

Servings: 8
Cooking Time: 15 Mins.

Directions:

1. Preheat the air fryer to 300°F.
2. Lightly spray an air-fryer-safe pan with olive oil; then place the pistachios, almonds, and walnuts inside the pan and place the pan inside the air fryer basket.
3. Cook for 15 minutes, shaking the basket every 5 Mins. to rotate the nuts.
4. While the nuts are roasting, boil the water in a small pan and stir in the honey and oil. Continue to stir while cooking until the water begins to evaporate and a thick sauce is formed. Note: The sauce should stick to the back of a wooden spoon when mixed. Turn off the heat.
5. Remove the nuts from the air fryer (cooking should have just completed) and spoon the nuts into the stovetop pan. Use a spatula to coat the nuts with the honey syrup.
6. Line a baking sheet with parchment paper and spoon the nuts onto the sheet. Lightly sprinkle the sugar and salt over the nuts and let cool in the refrigerator for at least 2 hours.
7. When the honey and sugar have hardened, store the nuts in an airtight container in the refrigerator.

Oreo-coated Peanut Butter Cups

Ingredients:

- 8 Standard ¾-ounce peanut butter cups, frozen
- ⅓ C. All-purpose flour
- 2 Large egg white(s), beaten until foamy
- 16 Oreos or other creme-filled chocolate sandwich cookies, ground to crumbs in a food processor
- Vegetable oil spray

Servings: 8
Cooking Time:
4 Mins.

Directions:

1. Set up and fill three shallow soup plates or small pie plates on your counter: one for the flour, one for the beaten egg white(s), and one for the cookie crumbs.

2. Dip a frozen peanut butter C. in the flour, turning it to coat all sides. Shake off any excess, then set it in the beaten egg white(s). Turn it to coat all sides, then let any excess egg white slip back into the rest. Set the candy bar in the cookie crumbs. Turn to coat on all parts, even the sides. Dip the peanut butter C. back in the egg white(s) as before, then into the cookie crumbs as before, making sure you have a solid, even coating all around the cup. Set aside while you dip and coat the remaining cups.

3. When all the peanut butter C. are dipped and coated, lightly coat them on all sides with the vegetable oil spray. Set them on a plate and freeze while the air fryer heats.

4. Preheat the air fryer to 400°F.

5. Set the dipped C. wider side up in the basket with as much air space between them as possible. Air-fry undisturbed for 4 minutes, or until they feel soft but the coating is set.

6. Turn off the machine and remove the basket from it. Set aside the basket with the fried C. for 10 minutes. Use a nonstick-safe spatula to transfer the fried C. to a wire rack. Cool for at least another 5 Mins. before serving.

POULTRY RECIPES

Coconut Chicken With Apricot-ginger Sauce

Ingredients:

- 1½ lb. boneless, skinless chicken tenders, cut in large chunks (about 1¼ inches)
- salt and pepper
- ½ C. cornstarch
- 2 eggs
- 1 tbsp. milk
- 3 C. shredded coconut (see below)
- oil for misting or cooking spray
- Apricot-Ginger Sauce
- ½ C. apricot preserves
- 2 tbsp. white vinegar
- ¼ tsp. ground ginger
- ¼ tsp. low-sodium soy sauce
- 2 tsp. white or yellow onion, grated or finely minced

Directions:

1. Mix all ingredients for the Apricot-Ginger Sauce well and let sit for flavors to blend while you cook the chicken.
2. Season chicken chunks with salt and pepper to taste.
3. Place cornstarch in a shallow dish.
4. In another shallow dish, beat together eggs and milk.
5. Place coconut in a third shallow dish. (If also using panko breadcrumbs, as suggested below, stir them to mix well.)
6. Spray air fryer basket with oil or cooking spray.
7. Dip each chicken chunk into cornstarch, shake off excess, and dip in egg mixture.
8. Shake off excess egg mixture and roll lightly in coconut or coconut mixture. Spray with oil.
9. Place coated chicken chunks in air fryer basket in a single layer, close together but without sides touching.
10. Cook at 360°F for 4minutes, stop, and turn chunks over.
11. Cook an additional 4 Mins. or until chicken is done inside and coating is crispy brown.
12. Repeat steps 9 through 11 to cook remaining chicken chunks.

Mediterranean Stuffed Chicken Breasts

Ingredients:

Servings: 4
Cooking Time:
24 Mins.

- 4 boneless, skinless chicken breasts
- ½ tsp. salt
- ½ tsp. black pepper
- ½ tsp. garlic powder
- ½ tsp. paprika
- ½ C. canned artichoke hearts, chopped
- 4 oz. cream cheese
- ¼ C. grated Parmesan cheese

Directions:

1. Pat the chicken breasts with a paper towel. Using a sharp knife, cut a pouch in the side of each chicken breast for filling.

2. In a small bowl, mix the salt, pepper, garlic powder, and paprika. Season the chicken breasts with this mixture.

3. In a medium bowl, mix together the artichokes, cream cheese, and grated Parmesan cheese. Divide the filling between the 4 breasts, stuffing it inside the pouches. Use toothpicks to close the pouches and secure the filling.

4. Preheat the air fryer to 360°F.

5. Spray the air fryer basket liberally with cooking spray, add the stuffed chicken breasts to the basket, and spray liberally with cooking spray again. Cook for 14 minutes, carefully turn over the chicken breasts, and cook another 10 minutes. Check the temperature at 20 Mins. cooking. Chicken breasts are fully cooked when the center measures 165°F. Cook in batches, if needed.

Chicken Adobo

Ingredients:

- 6 boneless chicken thighs
- ¼ C. soy sauce or tamari
- ½ C. rice wine vinegar
- 4 cloves garlic, minced
- ⅛ tsp. crushed red pepper flakes
- ½ tsp. black pepper

Directions:

1. Place the chicken thighs into a resealable plastic bag with the soy sauce or tamari, the rice wine vinegar, the garlic, and the crushed red pepper flakes. Seal the bag and let the chicken marinate at least 1 hour in the refrigerator.

2. Preheat the air fryer to 400°F.

3. Drain the chicken and pat dry with a paper towel. Season the chicken with black pepper and liberally spray with cooking spray.

4. Place the chicken in the air fryer basket and cook for 9 minutes, turn over at 9 Mins. and check for an internal temperature of 165°F, and cook another 3 minutes.

Buttermilk-fried Drumsticks

Ingredients:

Servings: 2
Cooking Time:
25 Mins.

- 1 egg
- ½ C. buttermilk
- ¾ C. self-rising flour
- ¾ C. seasoned panko breadcrumbs
- 1 tsp. salt
- ¼ tsp. ground black pepper (to mix into coating)
- 4 chicken drumsticks, skin on
- oil for misting or cooking spray

Directions:

1. Beat together egg and buttermilk in shallow dish.
2. In a second shallow dish, combine the flour, panko crumbs, salt, and pepper.
3. Sprinkle chicken legs with additional salt and pepper to taste.
4. Dip legs in buttermilk mixture, then roll in panko mixture, pressing in crumbs to make coating stick. Mist with oil or cooking spray.
5. Spray air fryer basket with cooking spray.
6. Cook drumsticks at 360°F for 10minutes. Turn pieces over and cook an additional 10minutes.
7. Turn pieces to check for browning. If you have any white spots that haven't begun to brown, spritz them with oil or cooking spray. Continue cooking for 5 more Mins. or until crust is golden brown and juices run clear. Larger, meatier drumsticks will take longer to cook than small ones.

Tortilla Crusted Chicken Breast

Ingredients:

- ⅓ C. flour
- 1 tsp. salt
- 1½ tsp. chili powder
- 1 tsp. ground cumin
- freshly ground black pepper
- 1 egg, beaten
- ¾ C. coarsely crushed yellow corn tortilla chips
- 2 (3- to 4-ounce) boneless chicken breasts
- vegetable oil
- ½ C. salsa
- ½ C. crumbled queso fresco
- fresh cilantro leaves
- sour cream or guacamole (optional)

Servings: 2
Cooking Time:
12 Mins.

Directions:

1. Set up a dredging station with three shallow dishes. Combine the flour, salt, chili powder, cumin and black pepper in the first shallow dish. Beat the egg in the second shallow dish. Place the crushed tortilla chips in the third shallow dish.

2. Dredge the chicken in the spiced flour, covering all sides of the breast. Then dip the chicken into the egg, coating the chicken completely. Finally, place the chicken into the tortilla chips and press the chips onto the chicken to make sure they adhere to all sides of the breast. Spray the coated chicken breasts on both sides with vegetable oil.

3. Preheat the air fryer to 380°F.

4. Air-fry the chicken for 6 minutes. Then turn the chicken breasts over and air-fry for another 6 minutes. (Increase the cooking time if you are using chicken breasts larger than 3 to 4 ounces.)

5. When the chicken has finished cooking, serve each breast with a little salsa, the crumbled queso fresco and cilantro as the finishing touch. Serve some sour cream and/or guacamole at the table, if desired.

Chicken Chimichangas

Ingredients:

- 2 C. cooked chicken, shredded
- 2 tbsp. chopped green chiles
- ½ tsp. oregano
- ½ tsp. cumin
- ½ tsp. onion powder
- ¼ tsp. garlic powder
- salt and pepper
- 8 flour tortillas (6- or 7-inch diameter)
- oil for misting or cooking spray
- Chimichanga Sauce
- 2 tbsp. butter
- 2 tbsp. flour
- 1 C. chicken broth
- ¼ C. light sour cream
- ¼ tsp. salt
- 2 oz. Pepper Jack or Monterey Jack cheese, shredded

Servings: 4
Cooking Time:
10 Mins.

Directions:

1. Make the sauce by melting butter in a saucepan over medium-low heat. Stir in flour until smooth and slightly bubbly. Gradually add broth, stirring constantly until smooth. Cook and stir 1 minute, until the mixture slightly thickens. Remove from heat and stir in sour cream and salt. Set aside.

2. In a medium bowl, mix together the chicken, chiles, oregano, cumin, onion powder, garlic, salt, and pepper. Stir in 3 to 4 tbsp. of the sauce, using just enough to make the filling moist but not soupy.

3. Divide filling among the 8 tortillas. Place filling down the center of tortilla, stopping about 1 inch from edges. Fold one side of tortilla over filling, fold the two sides in, and then roll up. Mist all sides with oil or cooking spray.

4. Place chimichangas in air fryer basket seam side down. To fit more into the basket, you can stand them on their sides with the seams against the sides of the basket.

5. Cook at 360°F for 10 Mins. or until heated through and crispy brown outside.

6. Add the shredded cheese to the remaining sauce. Stir over low heat, warming just until the cheese melts. Don't boil or sour cream may curdle.

7. Drizzle the sauce over the chimichangas.

Chicken Chunks

Ingredients:

- 1 lb. chicken tenders cut in large chunks, about 1½ inches
- salt and pepper
- ½ C. cornstarch
- 2 eggs, beaten
- 1 C. panko breadcrumbs
- oil for misting or cooking spray

Servings: 4
Cooking Time:
10 Mins.

Directions:

1. Season chicken chunks to your liking with salt and pepper.
2. Dip chicken chunks in cornstarch. Then dip in egg and shake off excess. Then roll in panko crumbs to coat well.
3. Spray all sides of chicken chunks with oil or cooking spray.
4. Place chicken in air fryer basket in single layer and cook at 390°F for 5minutes. Spray with oil, turn chunks over, and spray other side.
5. Cook for an additional 5minutes or until chicken juices run clear and outside is golden brown.
6. Repeat steps 4 and 5 to cook remaining chicken.

Parmesan Crusted Chicken Cordon Bleu

Ingredients:

- 2 (6-ounce) boneless, skinless chicken breasts
- salt and freshly ground black pepper
- 1 tbsp. Dijon mustard
- 4 slices Swiss cheese
- 4 slices deli-sliced ham
- ¼ C. all-purpose flour
- 1 egg, beaten
- ¾ C. panko breadcrumbs
- ⅓ C. grated Parmesan cheese
- olive oil, in a spray bottle

Servings: 2
Cooking Time: 14 Mins.

Directions:

1. Butterfly the chicken breasts. Place the chicken breast on a cutting board and press down on the breast with the palm of your hand. Slice into the long side of the chicken breast, parallel to the cutting board, but not all the way through to the other side. Open the chicken breast like a "book". Place a piece of plastic wrap over the chicken breast and gently lb. it with a meat mallet to make it evenly thick.

2. Season the chicken with salt and pepper. Spread the Dijon mustard on the inside of each chicken breast. Layer one slice of cheese on top of the mustard, then top with the 2 slices of ham and the other slice of cheese.

3. Starting with the long edge of the chicken breast, roll the chicken up to the other side. Secure it shut with 1 or 2 toothpicks.

4. Preheat the air fryer to 350°F.

5. Set up a dredging station with three shallow dishes. Place the flour in the first dish. Place the beaten egg in the second shallow dish. Combine the panko breadcrumbs and Parmesan cheese together in the third shallow dish. Dip the stuffed and rolled chicken breasts in the flour, then the beaten egg and then roll in the breadcrumb-cheese mixture to cover on all sides. Press the crumbs onto the chicken breasts with your hands to make sure they are well adhered. Spray the chicken breasts with olive oil and transfer to the air fryer basket.

6. Air-fry at 350°F for 14 minutes, flipping the breasts over halfway through the cooking time. Let the chicken rest for a few Mins. before removing the toothpicks, slicing and serving.

Chicken Hand Pies

Ingredients:

- ¾ C. chicken broth
- ¾ C. frozen mixed peas and carrots
- 1 C. cooked chicken, chopped
- 1 tbsp. cornstarch
- 1 tbsp. milk
- salt and pepper
- 1 8-count can organic flaky biscuits
- oil for misting or cooking spray

Directions:

1. In a medium saucepan, bring chicken broth to a boil. Stir in the frozen peas and carrots and cook for 5minutes over medium heat. Stir in chicken.

2. Mix the cornstarch into the milk until it dissolves. Stir it into the simmering chicken broth mixture and cook just until thickened.

3. Remove from heat, add salt and pepper to taste, and let cool slightly.

4. Lay biscuits out on wax paper. Peel each biscuit apart in the middle to make 2 rounds so you have 16 rounds total. Using your hands or a rolling pin, flatten each biscuit round slightly to make it larger and thinner.

5. Divide chicken filling among 8 of the biscuit rounds. Place remaining biscuit rounds on top and press edges all around. Use the tines of a fork to crimp biscuit edges and make sure they are sealed well.

6. Spray both sides lightly with oil or cooking spray.

7. Cook in a single layer, 4 at a time, at 330°F for 10minutes or until biscuit dough is cooked through and golden brown.

BEEF, PORK & LAMB RECIPES

Skirt Steak Fajitas

Ingredients:

Servings: 4
Cooking Time:
30 Mins.

- 2 tbsp. olive oil
- ¼ C. lime juice
- 1 clove garlic, minced
- ½ tsp. ground cumin
- ½ tsp. hot sauce
- ½ tsp. salt
- 2 tbsp. chopped fresh cilantro
- 1 lb. skirt steak
- 1 onion, sliced
- 1 tsp. chili powder
- 1 red pepper, sliced
- 1 green pepper, sliced
- salt and freshly ground black pepper
- 8 flour tortillas
- shredded lettuce, crumbled Queso Fresco (or grated Cheddar cheese), sliced black olives, diced tomatoes, sour cream and guacamole for serving

Directions:

1. Combine the olive oil, lime juice, garlic, cumin, hot sauce, salt and cilantro in a shallow dish. Add the skirt steak and turn it over several times to coat all sides. Pierce the steak with a needle-style meat tenderizer or paring knife. Marinate the steak in the refrigerator for at least 3 hours, or overnight. When you are ready to cook, remove the steak from the refrigerator and let it sit at room temperature for 30 minutes.

2. Preheat the air fryer to 400°F.

3. Toss the onion slices with the chili powder and a little olive oil and transfer them to the air fryer basket. Air-fry at 400°F for 5 minutes. Add the red and green peppers to the air fryer basket with the onions, season with salt and pepper and air-fry for 8 more minutes, until the onions and peppers are soft. Transfer the vegetables to a dish and cover with aluminum foil to keep warm.

4. Place the skirt steak in the air fryer basket and pour the marinade over the top. Air-fry at 400°F for 12 minutes. Flip the steak over and air-fry at 400°F for an additional 5 minutes. (The time needed for your steak will depend on the thickness of the skirt steak. 17 Mins. should bring your steak to roughly medium.) Transfer the cooked steak to a cutting board and let the steak rest for a few minutes. If the peppers and onions need to be heated, return them to the air fryer for just 1 to 2 minutes.

5. Thinly slice the steak at an angle, cutting against the grain of the steak. Serve the steak with the onions and peppers, the warm tortillas and the fajita toppings on the side so that everyone can make their own fajita.

Fried Spam

Ingredients:

- ½ C. All-purpose flour or gluten-free all-purpose flour
- 1 Large egg(s)
- 1 tbsp. Wasabi paste
- 1⅓ C. Plain panko bread crumbs (gluten-free, if a concern)
- 4 ½-inch-thick Spam slices
- Vegetable oil spray

Servings: 2
Cooking Time:
12 Mins.

Directions:

1. Preheat the air fryer to 400°F.
2. Set up and fill three shallow soup plates or small pie plates on your counter: one for the flour; one for the egg(s), whisked with the wasabi paste until uniform; and one for the bread crumbs.
3. Dip a slice of Spam in the flour, coating both sides. Slip it into the egg mixture and turn to coat on both sides, even along the edges. Let any excess egg mixture slip back into the rest, then set the slice in the bread crumbs. Turn it several times, pressing gently to make an even coating on both sides. Generously coat both sides of the slice with vegetable oil spray. Set aside so you can dip, coat, and spray the remaining slice(s).
4. Set the slices in the basket in a single layer so that they don't touch (even if they're close together). Air-fry undisturbed for 12 minutes, or until very brown and quite crunchy.
5. Use kitchen tongs to transfer the slices to a wire rack. Cool for a minute or two before serving.

Carne Asada

Ingredients:

- 4 cloves garlic, minced
- 3 chipotle peppers in adobo, chopped
- ⅓ C. chopped fresh parsley
- ⅓ C. chopped fresh oregano
- 1 tsp. ground cumin seed
- juice of 2 limes
- ⅓ C. olive oil
- 1 to 1½ lb. flank steak (depending on your appetites)
- salt
- tortillas and guacamole (optional – for serving)

Directions:

1. Make the marinade: Combine the garlic, chipotle, parsley, oregano, cumin, lime juice and olive oil in a non-reactive bowl. Coat the flank steak with the marinade and let it marinate for 30 Mins. to 8 hours. (Don't leave the steak out of refrigeration for longer than 2 hours, however.)
2. Preheat the air fryer to 390°F.
3. Remove the steak from the marinade and place it in the air fryer basket. Season the steak with salt and air-fry for 15 minutes, turning the steak over halfway through the cooking time and seasoning again with salt. This should cook the steak to medium. Add or subtract two Mins. for medium-well or medium-rare.
4. Remember to let the steak rest before slicing the meat against the grain. Serve with warm tortillas, guacamole and a fresh salsa like the Tomato-Corn Salsa below.

Pork Cutlets With Almond-lemon Crust

Ingredients:

- ¾ C. Almond flour
- ¾ C. Plain dried bread crumbs (gluten-free, if a concern)
- 1½ tsp. Finely grated lemon zest
- 1¼ tsp. Table salt
- ¾ tsp. Garlic powder
- ¾ tsp. Dried oregano
- 1 Large egg white(s)
- 2 tbsp. Water
- 3 6-ounce center-cut boneless pork loin chops (about ¾ inch thick)
- Olive oil spray

Directions:

1. Preheat the air fryer to 375°F .
2. Mix the almond flour, bread crumbs, lemon zest, salt, garlic powder, and dried oregano in a large bowl until well combined.
3. Whisk the egg white(s) and water in a shallow soup plate or small pie plate until uniform.
4. Dip a chop in the egg white mixture, turning it to coat all sides, even the ends. Let any excess egg white mixture slip back into the rest, then set it in the almond flour mixture. Turn it several times, pressing gently to coat it evenly. Generously coat the chop with olive oil spray, then set aside to dip and coat the remaining chop(s).
5. Set the chops in the basket with as much air space between them as possible. Air-fry undisturbed for 12 minutes, or until browned and crunchy. You may need to add 2 Mins. to the cooking time if the machine is at 360°F.
6. Use kitchen tongs to transfer the chops to a wire rack. Cool for a few Mins. before serving.

Lamb Koftas Meatballs

Ingredients:

- 1 lb. ground lamb
- 1 tsp. ground cumin
- 1 tsp. ground coriander
- 2 tbsp. chopped fresh mint
- 1 egg, beaten
- ½ tsp. salt
- freshly ground black pepper

**Servings: 3
Cooking Time:
8 Mins.**

Directions:

1. Combine all ingredients in a bowl and mix together well. Divide the mixture into 10 portions. Roll each portion into a ball and then by cupping the meatball in your hand, shape it into an oval.
2. Preheat the air fryer to 400°F.
3. Air-fry the koftas for 8 minutes.
4. Serve warm with the cucumber-yogurt dip.

Sweet Potato–crusted Pork Rib Chops

Ingredients:

- 2 Large egg white(s), well beaten
- 1½ C. (about 6 ounces) Crushed sweet potato chips (certified gluten-free, if a concern)
- 1 tsp. Ground cinnamon
- 1 tsp. Ground dried ginger
- 1 tsp. Table salt (optional)
- 2 10-ounce, 1-inch-thick bone-in pork rib chop(s)

Servings: 2
Cooking Time: 14 Mins.

Directions:

1. Preheat the air fryer to 375°F .

2. Set up and fill two shallow soup plates or small pie plates on your counter: one for the beaten egg white(s); and one for the crushed chips, mixed with the cinnamon, ginger, and salt (if using).

3. Dip a chop in the egg white(s), coating it on both sides as well as the edges. Let the excess egg white slip back into the rest, then set it in the crushed chip mixture. Turn it several times, pressing gently, until evenly coated on both sides and the edges. If necessary, set the chop aside and coat the remaining chop(s).

4. Set the chop(s) in the basket with as much air space between them as possible. Air-fry undisturbed for 12 minutes, or until crunchy and browned and an instant-read meat thermometer inserted into the center of a chop (without touching bone) registers 145°F. If the machine is at 360°F, you may need to add 2 Mins. to the cooking time.

5. Use kitchen tongs to transfer the chop(s) to a wire rack. Cool for 2 or 3 Mins. before serving.

Spicy Hoisin Bbq Pork Chops

Ingredients:

- 3 tbsp. hoisin sauce
- ¼ C. honey
- 1 tbsp. soy sauce
- 3 tbsp. rice vinegar
- 2 tbsp. brown sugar
- 1½ tsp. grated fresh ginger
- 1 to 2 tsp. Sriracha sauce, to taste
- 2 to 3 bone-in center cut pork chops, 1-inch thick (about 1¼ pounds)
- chopped scallions, for garnish

**Servings: 2
Cooking Time:
12 Mins.**

Directions:

1. Combine the hoisin sauce, honey, soy sauce, rice vinegar, brown sugar, ginger, and Sriracha sauce in a small saucepan. Whisk the ingredients together and bring the mixture to a boil over medium-high heat on the stovetop. Reduce the heat and simmer the sauce until it has reduced in volume and thickened slightly – about 10 minutes.

2. Preheat the air fryer to 400°F.

3. Place the pork chops into the air fryer basket and pour half the hoisin BBQ sauce over the top. Air-fry for 6 minutes. Then, flip the chops over, pour the remaining hoisin BBQ sauce on top and air-fry for 6 more minutes, depending on the thickness of the pork chops. The internal temperature of the pork chops should be 155°F when tested with an instant read thermometer.

4. Let the pork chops rest for 5 Mins. before serving. You can spoon a little of the sauce from the bottom drawer of the air fryer over the top if desired. Sprinkle with chopped scallions and serve.

Meatball Subs

Ingredients:

- Marinara Sauce
- 1 15-ounce can diced tomatoes
- 1 tsp. garlic powder
- 1 tsp. dried basil
- ½ tsp. oregano
- ⅛ tsp. salt
- 1 tbsp. robust olive oil
- Meatballs
- ¼ lb. ground turkey
- ¾ lb. very lean ground beef
- 1 tbsp. milk
- ½ C. torn bread pieces
- 1 egg
- ¼ tsp. salt
- ½ tsp. dried onion
- 1 tsp. garlic powder
- ¼ tsp. smoked paprika
- ¼ tsp. crushed red pepper
- 1½ tsp. dried parsley
- ¼ tsp. oregano
- 2 tsp. Worcestershire sauce
- Sandwiches
- 4 large whole-grain sub or hoagie rolls, split
- toppings, sliced or chopped:
- mushrooms
- jalapeño or banana peppers
- red or green bell pepper
- red onions
- grated cheese

**Servings: 4
Cooking Time:
11 Mins.**

Directions:

1. Place all marinara ingredients in saucepan and bring to a boil. Lower heat and simmer 10minutes, uncovered.
2. Combine all meatball ingredients in large bowl and stir. Mixture should be well blended but don't overwork it. Excessive mixing will toughen the meatballs.
3. Divide meat into 16 equal portions and shape into balls.
4. Cook the balls at 360°F until meat is done and juices run clear, about 11 minutes.
5. While meatballs are cooking, taste marinara. If you prefer stronger flavors, add more seasoning and simmer another 5minutes.
6. When meatballs finish cooking, drain them on paper towels.
7. To assemble subs, place 4 meatballs on each sub roll, spoon sauce over meat, and add preferred toppings. Serve with additional marinara for dipping.

Mongolian Beef

Ingredients:

- 1½ lb. flank steak, thinly sliced
- on the bias into ¼-inch strips
- Marinade
- 2 tbsp. soy sauce
- 1 clove garlic, smashed
- big pinch crushed red pepper flakes
- Sauce
- 1 tbsp. vegetable oil
- 2 cloves garlic, minced
- 1 tbsp. finely grated fresh ginger
- 3 dried red chili peppers
- ¾ C. soy sauce
- ¾ C. chicken stock
- 5 to 6 tbsp. brown sugar (depending on how sweet you want the sauce)
- ½ C. cornstarch, divided
- 1 bunch scallions, sliced into 2-inch pieces

**Servings: 4
Cooking Time:
15 Mins.**

Directions:

1. Marinate the beef in the soy sauce, garlic and red pepper flakes for one hour.

2. In the meantime, make the sauce. Preheat a small saucepan over medium heat on the stovetop. Add the oil, garlic, ginger and dried chili peppers and sauté for just a minute or two. Add the soy sauce, chicken stock and brown sugar and continue to simmer for a few minutes. Dissolve 3 tbsp. of cornstarch in 3 tbsp. of water and stir this into the saucepan. Stir the sauce over medium heat until it thickens. Set this aside.

3. Preheat the air fryer to 400°F.

4. Remove the beef from the marinade and transfer it to a zipper sealable plastic bag with the remaining cornstarch. Shake it around to completely coat the beef and transfer the coated strips of beef to a baking sheet or plate, shaking off any excess cornstarch. Spray the strips with vegetable oil on all sides and transfer them to the air fryer basket.

5. Air-fry at 400°F for 15 minutes, shaking the basket to toss and rotate the beef strips throughout the cooking process. Add the scallions for the last 4 Mins. of the cooking. Transfer the hot beef strips and scallions to a bowl and toss with the sauce (warmed on the stovetop if necessary), coating all the beef strips with the sauce. Serve warm over white rice.

FISH AND SEAFOOD RECIPES

Blackened Catfish

Ingredients:

- 1 tsp. paprika
- 1 tsp. garlic powder
- 1 tsp. onion powder
- 1 tsp. ground dried thyme
- ½ tsp. ground black pepper
- ⅛ tsp. cayenne pepper
- ½ tsp. dried oregano
- ⅛ tsp. crushed red pepper flakes
- 1 lb. catfish filets
- ½ tsp. sea salt
- 2 tbsp. butter, melted
- 1 tbsp. extra-virgin olive oil
- 2 tbsp. chopped parsley
- 1 lemon, cut into wedges

Servings: 4
Cooking Time: 8 Mins.

Directions:

1. In a small bowl, stir together the paprika, garlic powder, onion powder, thyme, black pepper, cayenne pepper, oregano, and crushed red pepper flakes.
2. Pat the fish dry with paper towels. Season the filets with sea salt and then coat with the blackening seasoning.
3. In a small bowl, mix together the butter and olive oil and drizzle over the fish filets, flipping them to coat them fully.
4. Preheat the air fryer to 350°F.
5. Place the fish in the air fryer basket and cook for 8 minutes, checking the fish for doneness after 4 minutes. The fish will flake easily when cooked.
6. Remove the fish from the air fryer. Top with chopped parsley and serve with lemon wedges.

Fish Sticks For Kids

Ingredients:

- 8 oz. fish fillets (pollock or cod)
- salt (optional)
- ½ C. plain breadcrumbs
- oil for misting or cooking spray

Directions:

1. Cut fish fillets into "fingers" about ½ x 3 inches. Sprinkle with salt to taste, if desired.
2. Roll fish in breadcrumbs. Spray all sides with oil or cooking spray.
3. Place in air fryer basket in single layer and cook at 390°F for 6 minutes, until golden brown and crispy.

Garlic And Dill Salmon

Ingredients:

Servings: 2
Cooking Time:
8 Mins.

- 12 oz. salmon filets with skin
- 2 tbsp. melted butter
- 1 tbsp. extra-virgin olive oil
- 2 garlic cloves, minced
- 1 tbsp. fresh dill
- ½ tsp. sea salt
- ½ lemon

Directions:

1. Pat the salmon dry with paper towels.
2. In a small bowl, mix together the melted butter, olive oil, garlic, and dill.
3. Sprinkle the top of the salmon with sea salt. Brush all sides of the salmon with the garlic and dill butter.
4. Preheat the air fryer to 350°F.
5. Place the salmon, skin side down, in the air fryer basket. Cook for 6 to 8 minutes, or until the fish flakes in the center.
6. Remove the salmon and plate on a serving platter. Squeeze fresh lemon over the top of the salmon. Serve immediately.

Crabmeat-stuffed Flounder

Ingredients:

Servings: 3
Cooking Time:
12 Mins.

- 4½ oz. Purchased backfin or claw crabmeat, picked over for bits of shell and cartilage
- 6 Saltine crackers, crushed into fine crumbs
- 2 tbsp. plus 1 tsp. Regular or low-fat mayonnaise (not fat-free)
- ¾ tsp. Yellow prepared mustard
- 1½ tsp. Worcestershire sauce
- ⅛ tsp. Celery salt
- 3 5- to 6-ounce skinless flounder fillets
- Vegetable oil spray
- Mild paprika

Directions:

1. Preheat the air fryer to 400°F.
2. Gently mix the crabmeat, crushed saltines, mayonnaise, mustard, Worcestershire sauce, and celery salt in a bowl until well combined.
3. Generously coat the flat side of a fillet with vegetable oil spray. Set the fillet sprayed side down on your work surface. Cut the fillet in half widthwise, then cut one of the halves in half lengthwise. Set a scant ⅓ C. of the crabmeat mixture on top of the undivided half of the fish fillet, mounding the mixture to make an oval that somewhat fits the shape of the fillet with at least a ¼-inch border of fillet beyond the filling all around.
4. Take the two thin divided quarters (that is, the halves of the half) and lay them lengthwise over the filling, overlapping at each end and leaving a little space in the middle where the filling peeks through. Coat the top of the stuffed flounder piece with vegetable oil spray, then sprinkle paprika over the stuffed flounder fillet. Set aside and use the remaining fillet(s) to make more stuffed flounder "packets," repeating steps 3 and
5. Use a nonstick-safe spatula to transfer the stuffed flounder fillets to the basket. Leave as much space between them as possible. Air-fry undisturbed for 12 minutes, or until lightly brown and firm (but not hard).
6. Use that same spatula, plus perhaps another one, to transfer the fillets to a serving platter or plates. Cool for a minute or two, then serve hot.

Crab Stuffed Salmon Roast

Ingredients:

- 1 (1½-pound) salmon fillet
- salt and freshly ground black pepper
- 6 oz. crabmeat
- 1 tsp. finely chopped lemon zest
- 1 tsp. Dijon mustard
- 1 tbsp. chopped fresh parsley, plus more for garnish
- 1 scallion, chopped
- ¼ tsp. salt
- olive oil

Servings: 4
Cooking Time: 20 Mins.

Directions:

1. Prepare the salmon fillet by butterflying it. Slice into the thickest side of the salmon, parallel to the countertop and along the length of the fillet. Don't slice all the way through to the other side – stop about an inch from the edge. Open the salmon up like a book. Season the salmon with salt and freshly ground black pepper.

2. Make the crab filling by combining the crabmeat, lemon zest, mustard, parsley, scallion, salt and freshly ground black pepper in a bowl. Spread this filling in the center of the salmon. Fold one side of the salmon over the filling. Then fold the other side over on top.

3. Transfer the rolled salmon to the center of a piece of parchment paper that is roughly 6- to 7-inches wide and about 12-inches long. The parchment paper will act as a sling, making it easier to put the salmon into the air fryer. Preheat the air fryer to 370°F. Use the parchment paper to transfer the salmon roast to the air fryer basket and tuck the ends of the paper down beside the salmon. Drizzle a little olive oil on top and season with salt and pepper.

4. Air-fry the salmon at 370°F for 20 minutes.

5. Remove the roast from the air fryer and let it rest for a few minutes. Then, slice it, sprinkle some more lemon zest and parsley (or fresh chives) on top and serve.

Pecan-crusted Tilapia

Ingredients:

- 1 lb. skinless, boneless tilapia filets
- ¼ C. butter, melted
- 1 tsp. minced fresh or dried rosemary
- 1 C. finely chopped pecans
- 1 tsp. sea salt
- ¼ tsp. paprika
- 2 tbsp. chopped parsley
- 1 lemon, cut into wedges

Servings: 4
Cooking Time: 8 Mins.

Directions:

1. Pat the tilapia filets dry with paper towels.
2. Pour the melted butter over the filets and flip the filets to coat them completely.
3. In a medium bowl, mix together the rosemary, pecans, salt, and paprika.
4. Preheat the air fryer to 350°F.
5. Place the tilapia filets into the air fryer basket and top with the pecan coating. Cook for 6 to 8 minutes. The fish should be firm to the touch and flake easily when fully cooked.
6. Remove the fish from the air fryer. Top the fish with chopped parsley and serve with lemon wedges.

Coconut-shrimp Po' Boys

Ingredients:

- ½ C. cornstarch
- 2 eggs
- 2 tbsp. milk
- ¾ C. shredded coconut
- ½ C. panko breadcrumbs
- 1 lb. (31–35 count) shrimp, peeled and deveined
- Old Bay Seasoning
- oil for misting or cooking spray
- 2 large hoagie rolls
- honey mustard or light mayonnaise
- 1½ C. shredded lettuce
- 1 large tomato, thinly sliced

Directions:

1. Place cornstarch in a shallow dish or plate.
2. In another shallow dish, beat together eggs and milk.
3. In a third dish mix the coconut and panko crumbs.
4. Sprinkle shrimp with Old Bay Seasoning to taste.
5. Dip shrimp in cornstarch to coat lightly, dip in egg mixture, shake off excess, and roll in coconut mixture to coat well.
6. Spray both sides of coated shrimp with oil or cooking spray.
7. Cook half the shrimp in a single layer at 390°F for 5minutes.
8. Repeat to cook remaining shrimp.
9. To Assemble
10. Split each hoagie lengthwise, leaving one long edge intact.
11. Place in air fryer basket and cook at 390°F for 1 to 2minutes or until heated through.
12. Remove buns, break apart, and place on 4 plates, cut side up.
13. Spread with honey mustard and/or mayonnaise.
14. Top with shredded lettuce, tomato slices, and coconut shrimp.

Horseradish Crusted Salmon

Ingredients:

- 2 (5-ounce) salmon fillets
- salt and freshly ground black pepper
- 2 tsp. Dijon mustard
- ½ C. panko breadcrumbs
- 2 tbsp. prepared horseradish
- ½ tsp. finely chopped lemon zest
- 1 tbsp. olive oil
- 1 tbsp. chopped fresh parsley

Servings: 2
Cooking Time:
14 Mins.

Directions:

1. Preheat the air fryer to 360°F.
2. Season the salmon with salt and freshly ground black pepper. Then spread the Dijon mustard on the salmon, coating the entire surface.
3. Combine the breadcrumbs, horseradish, lemon zest and olive oil in a small bowl. Spread the mixture over the top of the salmon and press down lightly with your hands, adhering it to the salmon using the mustard as "glue".
4. Transfer the salmon to the air fryer basket and air-fry at 360°F for 14 Mins. (depending on how thick your fillet is) or until the fish feels firm to the touch. Sprinkle with the parsley.

Stuffed Shrimp

Ingredients:

- 16 tail-on shrimp, peeled and deveined (last tail section intact)
- ¾ C. crushed panko breadcrumbs
- oil for misting or cooking spray
- Stuffing
- 2 6-ounce cans lump crabmeat
- 2 tbsp. chopped shallots
- 2 tbsp. chopped green onions
- 2 tbsp. chopped celery
- 2 tbsp. chopped green bell pepper
- ½ C. crushed saltine crackers
- 1 tsp. Old Bay Seasoning
- 1 tsp. garlic powder
- ¼ tsp. ground thyme
- 2 tsp. dried parsley flakes
- 2 tsp. fresh lemon juice
- 2 tsp. Worcestershire sauce
- 1 egg, beaten

Servings: 4
Cooking Time:
12 Mins.

Directions:

1. Rinse shrimp. Remove tail section (shell) from 4 shrimp, discard, and chop the meat finely.
2. To prepare the remaining 12 shrimp, cut a deep slit down the back side so that the meat lies open flat. Do not cut all the way through.
3. Preheat air fryer to 360°F.
4. Place chopped shrimp in a large bowl with all of the stuffing ingredients and stir to combine.
5. Divide stuffing into 12 portions, about 2 tbsp. each.
6. Place one stuffing portion onto the back of each shrimp and form into a ball or oblong shape. Press firmly so that stuffing sticks together and adheres to shrimp.
7. Gently roll each stuffed shrimp in panko crumbs and mist with oil or cooking spray.
8. Place 6 shrimp in air fryer basket and cook at 360°F for 10minutes. Mist with oil or spray and cook 2 Mins. longer or until stuffing cooks through inside and is crispy outside.
9. Repeat step 8 to cook remaining shrimp.

SANDWICHES AND BURGERS RECIPES

White Bean Veggie Burgers

Ingredients:

- 1⅓ C. Drained and rinsed canned white beans
- 3 tbsp. Rolled oats (not quick-cooking or steel-cut; gluten-free, if a concern)
- 3 tbsp. Chopped walnuts
- 2 tsp. Olive oil
- 2 tsp. Lemon juice
- 1½ tsp. Dijon mustard (gluten-free, if a concern)
- ¾ tsp. Dried sage leaves
- ¼ tsp. Table salt
- Olive oil spray
- 3 Whole-wheat buns or gluten-free whole-grain buns (if a concern), split open

Servings: 3
Cooking Time: 13 Mins.

Directions:

1. Preheat the air fryer to 400°F.
2. Place the beans, oats, walnuts, oil, lemon juice, mustard, sage, and salt in a food processor. Cover and process to make a coarse paste that will hold its shape, about like wet sugar-cookie dough, stopping the machine to scrape down the inside of the canister at least once.
3. Scrape down and remove the blade. With clean and wet hands, form the bean paste into two 4-inch patties for the small batch, three 4-inch patties for the medium, or four 4-inch patties for the large batch. Generously coat the patties on both sides with olive oil spray.
4. Set them in the basket with some space between them and air-fry undisturbed for 12 minutes, or until lightly brown and crisp at the edges. The tops of the burgers will feel firm to the touch.
5. Use a nonstick-safe spatula, and perhaps a flatware fork for balance, to transfer the burgers to a cutting board. Set the buns cut side down in the basket in one layer (working in batches as necessary) and air-fry undisturbed for 1 minute, to toast a bit and warm up. Serve the burgers warm in the buns.

Eggplant Parmesan Subs

Ingredients:

- 4 Peeled eggplant slices (about ½ inch thick and 3 inches in diameter)
- Olive oil spray
- 2 tbsp. plus 2 tsp. Jarred pizza sauce, any variety except creamy
- ¼ C. (about ⅔ ounce) Finely grated Parmesan cheese
- 2 Small, long soft rolls, such as hero, hoagie, or Italian sub rolls (gluten-free, if a concern), split open lengthwise

Servings: 2
Cooking Time:
13 Mins.

Directions:

1. Preheat the air fryer to 350°F .

2. When the machine is at temperature, coat both sides of the eggplant slices with olive oil spray. Set them in the basket in one layer and air-fry undisturbed for 10 minutes, until lightly browned and softened.

3. Increase the machine's temperature to 375°F (or 370°F, if that's the closest setting—unless the machine is already at 360°F, in which case leave it alone). Top each eggplant slice with 2 tsp. pizza sauce, then 1 tbsp. cheese. Air-fry undisturbed for 2 minutes, or until the cheese has melted.

4. Use a nonstick-safe spatula, and perhaps a flatware fork for balance, to transfer the eggplant slices cheese side up to a cutting board. Set the roll(s) cut side down in the basket in one layer (working in batches as necessary) and air-fry undisturbed for 1 minute, to toast the rolls a bit and warm them up. Set 2 eggplant slices in each warm roll.

Chicken Apple Brie Melt

Ingredients:

- 3 5- to 6-ounce boneless skinless chicken breasts
- Vegetable oil spray
- 1½ tsp. Dried herbes de Provence
- 3 oz. Brie, rind removed, thinly sliced
- 6 Thin cored apple slices
- 3 French rolls (gluten-free, if a concern)
- 2 tbsp. Dijon mustard (gluten-free, if a concern)

Servings: 3
Cooking Time:
13 Mins.

Directions:

1. Preheat the air fryer to 375°F .
2. Lightly coat all sides of the chicken breasts with vegetable oil spray. Sprinkle the breasts evenly with the herbes de Provence.
3. When the machine is at temperature, set the breasts in the basket and air-fry undisturbed for 10 minutes.
4. Top the chicken breasts with the apple slices, then the cheese. Air-fry undisturbed for 2 minutes, or until the cheese is melty and bubbling.
5. Use a nonstick-safe spatula and kitchen tongs, for balance, to transfer the breasts to a cutting board. Set the rolls in the basket and air-fry for 1 minute to warm through. (Putting them in the machine without splitting them keeps the insides very soft while the outside gets a little crunchy.)
6. Transfer the rolls to the cutting board. Split them open lengthwise, then spread 1 tsp. mustard on each cut side. Set a prepared chicken breast on the bottom of a roll and close with its top, repeating as necessary to make additional sandwiches. Serve warm.

Chicken Saltimbocca Sandwiches

Ingredients:

- 3 5- to 6-ounce boneless skinless chicken breasts
- 6 Thin prosciutto slices
- 6 Provolone cheese slices
- 3 Long soft rolls, such as hero, hoagie, or Italian sub rolls (gluten-free, if a concern), split open lengthwise
- 3 tbsp. Pesto, purchased or homemade (see the headnote)

Servings: 3
Cooking Time: 11 Mins.

Directions:

1. Preheat the air fryer to 400°F.
2. Wrap each chicken breast with 2 prosciutto slices, spiraling the prosciutto around the breast and overlapping the slices a bit to cover the breast. The prosciutto will stick to the chicken more readily than bacon does.
3. When the machine is at temperature, set the wrapped chicken breasts in the basket and air-fry undisturbed for 10 minutes, or until the prosciutto is frizzled and the chicken is cooked through.
4. Overlap 2 cheese slices on each breast. Air-fry undisturbed for 1 minute, or until melted. Take the basket out of the machine.
5. Smear the insides of the rolls with the pesto, then use kitchen tongs to put a wrapped and cheesy chicken breast in each roll.

Crunchy Falafel Balls

Ingredients:

- 2½ C. Drained and rinsed canned chickpeas
- ¼ C. Olive oil
- 3 tbsp. All-purpose flour
- 1½ tsp. Dried oregano
- 1½ tsp. Dried sage leaves
- 1½ tsp. Dried thyme
- ¾ tsp. Table salt
- Olive oil spray

Directions:

1. Preheat the air fryer to 400°F.
2. Place the chickpeas, olive oil, flour, oregano, sage, thyme, and salt in a food processor. Cover and process into a paste, stopping the machine at least once to scrape down the inside of the canister.
3. Scrape down and remove the blade. Using clean, wet hands, form 2 tbsp. of the paste into a ball, then continue making 9 more balls for a small batch, 15 more for a medium one, and 19 more for a large batch. Generously coat the balls in olive oil spray.
4. Set the balls in the basket in one layer with a little space between them and air-fry undisturbed for 16 minutes, or until well browned and crisp.
5. Dump the contents of the basket onto a wire rack. Cool for 5 Mins. before serving.

Turkey Burgers

Ingredients:

- 1 lb. 2 oz. Ground turkey
- 6 tbsp. Frozen chopped spinach, thawed and squeezed dry
- 3 tbsp. Plain panko bread crumbs (gluten-free, if a concern)
- 1 tbsp. Dijon mustard (gluten-free, if a concern)
- 1½ tsp. Minced garlic
- ¾ tsp. Table salt
- ¾ tsp. Ground black pepper
- Olive oil spray
- 3 Kaiser rolls (gluten-free, if a concern), split open

Servings: 3
Cooking Time:
23 Mins.

Directions:

1. Preheat the air fryer to 375°F .

2. Gently mix the ground turkey, spinach, bread crumbs, mustard, garlic, salt, and pepper in a large bowl until well combined, trying to keep some of the fibers of the ground turkey intact. Form into two 5-inch-wide patties for the small batch, three 5-inch patties for the medium batch, or four 5-inch patties for the large. Coat each side of the patties with olive oil spray.

3. Set the patties in in the basket in one layer and air-fry undisturbed for 20 minutes, or until an instant-read meat thermometer inserted into the center of a burger registers 165°F. You may need to add 2 Mins. to the cooking time if the air fryer is at 360°F.

4. Use a nonstick-safe spatula, and perhaps a flatware fork for balance, to transfer the burgers to a cutting board. Set the buns cut side down in the basket in one layer (working in batches as necessary) and air-fry for 1 minute, to toast a bit and warm up. Serve the burgers warm in the buns.

Mexican Cheeseburgers

Ingredients:

Servings: 4
Cooking Time:
22 Mins.

- 1¼ lb. ground beef
- ¼ C. finely chopped onion
- ½ C. crushed yellow corn tortilla chips
- 1 (1.25-ounce) packet taco seasoning
- ¼ C. canned diced green chilies
- 1 egg, lightly beaten
- 4 oz. pepper jack cheese, grated
- 4 (12-inch) flour tortillas
- shredded lettuce, sour cream, guacamole, salsa (for topping)

Directions:

1. Combine the ground beef, minced onion, crushed tortilla chips, taco seasoning, green chilies, and egg in a large bowl. Mix thoroughly until combined – your hands are good tools for this. Divide the meat into four equal portions and shape each portion into an oval-shaped burger.

2. Preheat the air fryer to 370°F.

3. Air-fry the burgers for 18 minutes, turning them over halfway through the cooking time. Divide the cheese between the burgers, lower fryer to 340°F and air-fry for an additional 4 Mins. to melt the cheese. (This will give you a burger that is medium-well. If you prefer your cheeseburger medium-rare, shorten the cooking time to about 15 Mins. and then add the cheese and proceed with the recipe.)

4. While the burgers are cooking, warm the tortillas wrapped in aluminum foil in a 350°F oven, or in a skillet with a little oil over medium-high heat for a couple of minutes. Keep the tortillas warm until the burgers are ready.

5. To assemble the burgers, spread sour cream over three quarters of the tortillas and top each with some shredded lettuce and salsa. Place the Mexican cheeseburgers on the lettuce and top with guacamole. Fold the tortillas around the burger, starting with the bottom and then folding the sides in over the top. (A little sour cream can help hold the seam of the tortilla together.) Serve immediately.

Dijon Thyme Burgers

Ingredients:

- 1 lb. lean ground beef
- ⅓ C. panko breadcrumbs
- ¼ C. finely chopped onion
- 3 tbsp. Dijon mustard
- 1 tbsp. chopped fresh thyme
- 4 tsp. Worcestershire sauce
- 1 tsp. salt
- freshly ground black pepper
- Topping (optional):
- 2 tbsp. Dijon mustard
- 1 tbsp. dark brown sugar
- 1 tsp. Worcestershire sauce
- 4 oz. sliced Swiss cheese, optional

Servings: 3
Cooking Time: 18 Mins.

Directions:

1. Combine all the burger ingredients together in a large bowl and mix well. Divide the meat into 4 equal portions and then form the burgers, being careful not to over-handle the meat. One good way to do this is to throw the meat back and forth from one hand to another, packing the meat each time you catch it. Flatten the balls into patties, making an indentation in the center of each patty with your thumb (this will help it stay flat as it cooks) and flattening the sides of the burgers so that they will fit nicely into the air fryer basket.
2. Preheat the air fryer to 370°F.
3. If you don't have room for all four burgers, air-fry two or three burgers at a time for 8 minutes. Flip the burgers over and air-fry for another 6 minutes.
4. While the burgers are cooking combine the Dijon mustard, dark brown sugar, and Worcestershire sauce in a small bowl and mix well. This optional topping to the burgers really adds a boost of flavor at the end. Spread the Dijon topping evenly on each burger. If you cooked the burgers in batches, return the first batch to the cooker at this time – it's ok to place the fourth burger on top of the others in the center of the basket. Air-fry the burgers for another 3 minutes.
5. Finally, if desired, top each burger with a slice of Swiss cheese. Lower the air fryer temperature to 330°F and air-fry for another minute to melt the cheese. Serve the burgers on toasted brioche buns, dressed the way you like them.

Salmon Burgers

Ingredients:

- 1 lb. 2 oz. Skinless salmon fillet, preferably fattier Atlantic salmon
- 1½ tbsp. Minced chives or the green part of a scallion
- ½ C. Plain panko bread crumbs (gluten-free, if a concern)
- 1½ tsp. Dijon mustard (gluten-free, if a concern)
- 1½ tsp. Drained and rinsed capers, minced
- 1½ tsp. Lemon juice
- ¼ tsp. Table salt
- ¼ tsp. Ground black pepper
- Vegetable oil spray

Servings: 3
Cooking Time:
8 Mins.

Directions:

1. Preheat the air fryer to 375°F .

2. Cut the salmon into pieces that will fit in a food processor. Cover and pulse until coarsely chopped. Add the chives and pulse to combine, until the fish is ground but not a paste. Scrape down and remove the blade. Scrape the salmon mixture into a bowl. Add the bread crumbs, mustard, capers, lemon juice, salt, and pepper. Stir gently until well combined.

3. Use clean and dry hands to form the mixture into two 5-inch patties for a small batch, three 5-inch patties for a medium batch, or four 5-inch patties for a large one.

4. Coat both sides of each patty with vegetable oil spray. Set them in the basket in one layer and air-fry undisturbed for 8 minutes, or until browned and an instant-read meat thermometer inserted into the center of a burger registers 145°F.

5. Use a nonstick-safe spatula, and perhaps a flatware fork for balance, to transfer the burgers to a wire rack. Cool for 2 or 3 Mins. before serving.

Root Vegetable Crisps

Ingredients:

- 1 small taro root, peeled and washed
- 1 small yucca root, peeled and washed
- 1 small purple sweet potato, washed
- 2 C. filtered water
- 2 tsp. extra-virgin olive oil
- ½ tsp. salt

Servings: 4
Cooking Time:
8 Mins.

Directions:

1. Using a mandolin, slice the taro root, yucca root, and purple sweet potato into ⅛-inch slices.
2. Add the water to a large bowl. Add the sliced vegetables and soak for at least 30 minutes.
3. Preheat the air fryer to 370°F.
4. Drain the water and pat the vegetables dry with a paper towel or kitchen cloth. Toss the vegetables with the olive oil and sprinkle with salt. Liberally spray the air fryer basket with olive oil mist.
5. Place the vegetables into the air fryer basket, making sure not to overlap the pieces.
6. Cook for 8 minutes, shaking the basket every 2 minutes, until the outer edges start to turn up and the vegetables start to brown. Remove from the basket and serve warm. Repeat with the remaining vegetable slices until all are cooked.

Caponata Salsa

Ingredients:

- 4 C. (one 1-pound eggplant) Purple Italian eggplant(s), stemmed and diced (no need to peel)
- Olive oil spray
- 1½ C. Celery, thinly sliced
- 16 (about ½ pound) Cherry or grape tomatoes, halved
- 1 tbsp. Drained and rinsed capers, chopped
- Up to 1 tbsp. Minced fresh rosemary leaves
- 1½ tbsp. Red wine vinegar
- 1½ tsp. Granulated white sugar
- ¾ tsp. Table salt
- ¾ tsp. Ground black pepper

Servings: 6
Cooking Time:
16 Mins.

Directions:

1. Preheat the air fryer to 350°F .

2. Put the eggplant pieces in a bowl and generously coat them with olive oil spray. Toss and stir, spray again, and toss some more, until the pieces are glistening.

3. When the machine is at temperature, pour the eggplant pieces into the basket and spread them out into an even layer. Air-fry for 8 minutes, tossing and rearranging the pieces twice.

4. Meanwhile, put the celery and tomatoes in the same bowl the eggplant pieces had been in. Generously coat them with olive oil spray; then toss well, spray again, and toss some more, until the vegetables are well coated.

5. When the eggplant has cooked for 8 minutes, pour the celery and tomatoes on top in the basket. Air-fry undisturbed for 8 Mins. more, until the tomatoes have begun to soften.

6. Pour the contents of the basket back into the same bowl. Add the capers, rosemary, vinegar, sugar, salt, and pepper. Toss well to blend, breaking up the tomatoes a bit to create more moisture in the mixture.

7. Cover and refrigerate for 2 hours to blend the flavors. Serve chilled or at room temperature. The caponata salsa can stay in its covered bowl in the fridge for up to 2 days before the vegetables weep too much moisture and the dish becomes too wet.

Fried Dill Pickle Chips

Ingredients:

- 1 C. All-purpose flour or tapioca flour
- 1 Large egg white(s)
- 1 tbsp. Brine from a jar of dill pickles
- 1 C. Seasoned Italian-style dried bread crumbs (gluten-free, if a concern)
- 2 Large dill pickle(s) (8 to 10 inches long), cut into ½-inch-thick rounds
- Vegetable oil spray

Servings: 4
Cooking Time:
12 Mins.

Directions:

1. Preheat the air fryer to 400°F.
2. Set up and fill three shallow soup plates or small pie plates on your counter: one for the flour, one for the egg white(s) whisked with the pickle brine, and one for the bread crumbs.
3. Set a pickle round in the flour and turn it to coat all sides, even the edge. Gently shake off the excess flour, then dip the round into the egg-white mixture and turn to coat both sides and the edge. Let any excess egg white mixture slip back into the rest, then set the round in the bread crumbs and turn it to coat both sides as well as the edge. Set aside on a cutting board and soldier on, dipping and coating the remaining rounds. Lightly coat the coated rounds on both sides with vegetable oil spray.
4. Set the pickle rounds in the basket in one layer. Air-fry undisturbed for 7 minutes, or until golden brown and crunchy. Cool in the basket for a few Mins. before using kitchen tongs to transfer the (still hot) rounds to a serving platter.

Grilled Ham & Muenster Cheese On Raisin Bread

Ingredients:

- 2 slices raisin bread
- 2 tbsp. butter, softened
- 2 tsp. honey mustard
- 3 slices thinly sliced honey ham (about 3 ounces)
- 4 slices Muenster cheese (about 3 ounces)
- 2 toothpicks

Servings: 1
Cooking Time:
10 Mins.

Directions:

1. Preheat the air fryer to 370°F.
2. Spread the softened butter on one side of both slices of raisin bread and place the bread, buttered side down on the counter. Spread the honey mustard on the other side of each slice of bread. Layer 2 slices of cheese, the ham and the remaining 2 slices of cheese on one slice of bread and top with the other slice of bread. Remember to leave the buttered side of the bread on the outside.
3. Transfer the sandwich to the air fryer basket and secure the sandwich with toothpicks.
4. Air-fry at 370°F for 5 minutes. Flip the sandwich over, remove the toothpicks and air-fry for another 5 minutes. Cut the sandwich in half and enjoy!!

Zucchini Fritters

Ingredients:

- 2 C. grated zucchini
- ½ tsp. sea salt
- 1 egg
- ½ tsp. garlic powder
- ¼ tsp. onion powder
- ¼ C. grated Parmesan cheese
- ½ C. all-purpose flour
- ¼ tsp. baking powder
- ½ C. Greek yogurt or sour cream
- ½ lime, juiced
- ¼ C. chopped cilantro
- ¼ tsp. ground cumin
- ¼ tsp. salt

**Servings: 8
Cooking Time:
10 Mins.**

Directions:

1. Preheat the air fryer to 360°F.

2. In a large colander, place a kitchen towel. Inside the towel, place the grated zucchini and sprinkle the sea salt over the top. Let the zucchini sit for 5 minutes; then, using the towel, squeeze dry the zucchini.

3. In a medium bowl, mix together the egg, garlic powder, onion powder, Parmesan cheese, flour, and baking powder. Add in the grated zucchini, and stir until completely combined.

4. Pierce a piece of parchment paper with a fork 4 to 6 times. Place the parchment paper into the air fryer basket. Using a tablespoon, place 6 to 8 heaping tbsp. of fritter batter onto the parchment paper. Spray the fritters with cooking spray and cook for 5 minutes, turn the fritters over, and cook another 5 minutes.

5. Meanwhile, while the fritters are cooking, make the sauce. In a small bowl, whisk together the Greek yogurt or sour cream, lime juice, cilantro, cumin, and salt.

6. Repeat Steps 2–4 with the remaining batter.

Cheesy Pigs In A Blanket

Ingredients:

- 24 cocktail size smoked sausages
- 6 slices deli-sliced Cheddar cheese, each cut into 8 rectangular pieces
- 1 (8-ounce) tube refrigerated crescent roll dough
- ketchup or mustard for dipping

Directions:

1. Unroll the crescent roll dough into one large sheet. If your crescent roll dough has perforated seams, pinch or roll all the perforated seams together. Cut the large sheet of dough into 4 rectangles. Then cut each rectangle into 6 pieces by making one slice lengthwise in the middle and 2 slices horizontally. You should have 24 pieces of dough.

2. Make a deep slit lengthwise down the center of the cocktail sausage. Stuff two pieces of cheese into the slit in the sausage. Roll one piece of crescent dough around the stuffed cocktail sausage leaving the ends of the sausage exposed. Pinch the seam together. Repeat with the remaining sausages.

3. Preheat the air fryer to 350°F.

4. Air-fry in 2 batches, placing the sausages seam side down in the basket. Air-fry for 7 minutes. Serve hot with ketchup or your favorite mustard for dipping.

Cuban Sliders

Ingredients:

- 8 slices ciabatta bread, ¼-inch thick
- cooking spray
- 1 tbsp. brown mustard
- 6-8 oz. thin sliced leftover roast pork
- 4 oz. thin deli turkey
- ⅓ C. bread and butter pickle slices
- 2–3 oz. Pepper Jack cheese slices

Servings: 8
Cooking Time:
8 Mins.

Directions:

1. Spray one side of each slice of bread with butter or olive oil cooking spray.
2. Spread brown mustard on other side of each slice.
3. Layer pork roast, turkey, pickles, and cheese on 4 of the slices. Top with remaining slices.
4. Cook at 390°F for approximately 8minutes. The sandwiches should be golden brown.
5. Cut each slider in half to make 8 portions.

Herbed Cheese Brittle

Ingredients:

- ½ C. shredded Parmesan cheese
- ½ C. shredded white cheddar cheese
- 1 tbsp. fresh chopped rosemary
- 1 tsp. garlic powder
- 1 large egg white

Servings: 4
Cooking Time:
5 Mins.

Directions:

1. Preheat the air fryer to 400°F.
2. In a large bowl, mix the cheeses, rosemary, and garlic powder. Mix in the egg white. Then pour the batter into a 7-inch pan (or an air-fryer-compatible pan). Place the pan in the air fryer basket and cook for 4 to 5 minutes, or until the cheese is melted and slightly browned.
3. Remove the pan from the air fryer, and let it cool for 2 minutes. Invert the pan before the cheese brittle completely cools but is semi-hardened to allow it to easily slide out of the pan.
4. Let the pan cool another 5 minutes. Break into pieces and serve.

Cheese Straws

Ingredients:

- For dusting All-purpose flour
- Two quarters of one thawed sheet (that is, a half of the sheet cut into two even pieces; wrap and refreeze the remainder) A 17.25-ounce box frozen puff pastry
- 1 Large egg(s)
- 2 tbsp. Water
- ¼ C. (about ¾ ounce) Finely grated Parmesan cheese
- up to 1 tsp. Ground black pepper

Directions:

1. Preheat the air fryer to 400°F.
2. Dust a clean, dry work surface with flour. Set one of the pieces of puff pastry on top, dust the pastry lightly with flour, and roll with a rolling pin to a 6-inch square.
3. Whisk the egg(s) and water in a small or medium bowl until uniform. Brush the pastry square(s) generously with this mixture. Sprinkle each square with 2 tbsp. grated cheese and up to ½ tsp. ground black pepper.
4. Cut each square into 4 even strips. Grasp each end of 1 strip with clean, dry hands; twist it into a cheese straw. Place the twisted straws on a baking sheet.
5. Lay as many straws as will fit in the air-fryer basket—as a general rule, 4 of them in a small machine, 5 in a medium model, or 6 in a large. There should be space for air to circulate around the straws. Set the baking sheet with any remaining straws in the fridge.
6. Air-fry undisturbed for 7 minutes, or until puffed and crisp. Use tongs to transfer the cheese straws to a wire rack, then make subsequent batches in the same way (keeping the baking sheet with the remaining straws in the fridge as each batch cooks). Serve warm.

VEGETARIANS RECIPES

Vegetable Couscous

Ingredients:

- 4 oz. white mushrooms, sliced
- ½ medium green bell pepper, julienned
- 1 C. cubed zucchini
- ¼ small onion, slivered
- 1 stalk celery, thinly sliced
- ¼ tsp. ground coriander
- ¼ tsp. ground cumin
- salt and pepper
- 1 tbsp. olive oil
- Couscous
- ¾ C. uncooked couscous
- 1 C. vegetable broth or water
- ½ tsp. salt (omit if using salted broth)

Directions:

1. Combine all vegetables in large bowl. Sprinkle with coriander, cumin, and salt and pepper to taste. Stir well, add olive oil, and stir again to coat vegetables evenly.
2. Place vegetables in air fryer basket and cook at 390°F for 5minutes. Stir and cook for 5 more minutes, until tender.
3. While vegetables are cooking, prepare the couscous: Place broth or water and salt in large saucepan. Heat to boiling, stir in couscous, cover, and remove from heat.
4. Let couscous sit for 5minutes, stir in cooked vegetables, and serve hot.

Lentil Fritters

Ingredients:

- 1 C. cooked red lentils
- 1 C. riced cauliflower
- ½ medium zucchini, shredded (about 1 cup)
- ¼ C. finely chopped onion
- ¼ tsp. salt
- ¼ tsp. black pepper
- ½ tsp. garlic powder
- ¼ tsp. paprika
- 1 large egg
- ⅓ C. quinoa flour

Servings: 9
Cooking Time:
12 Mins.

Directions:

1. Preheat the air fryer to 370°F.
2. In a large bowl, mix the lentils, cauliflower, zucchini, onion, salt, pepper, garlic powder, and paprika. Mix in the egg and flour until a thick dough forms.
3. Using a large spoon, form the dough into 9 large fritters.
4. Liberally spray the air fryer basket with olive oil. Place the fritters into the basket, leaving space around each fritter so you can flip them.
5. Cook for 6 minutes, flip, and cook another 6 minutes.
6. Remove from the air fryer and repeat with the remaining fritters. Serve warm with desired sauce and sides.

Pinto Taquitos

Ingredients:

Servings: 4
Cooking Time:
8 Mins.

- 12 corn tortillas (6- to 7-inch size)
- Filling
- ½ C. refried pinto beans
- ½ C. grated sharp Cheddar or Pepper Jack cheese
- ¼ C. corn kernels (if frozen, measure after thawing and draining)
- 2 tbsp. chopped green onion
- 2 tbsp. chopped jalapeño pepper (seeds and ribs removed before chopping)
- ½ tsp. lime juice
- ½ tsp. chile powder, plus extra for dusting
- ½ tsp. cumin
- ½ tsp. garlic powder
- oil for misting or cooking spray
- salsa, sour cream, or guacamole for dipping

Directions:

1. Mix together all filling Ingredients.
2. Warm refrigerated tortillas for easier rolling. (Wrap in damp paper towels and microwave for 30 to 60 seconds.)
3. Working with one at a time, place 1 tbsp. of filling on tortilla and roll up. Spray with oil or cooking spray and dust outside with chile powder to taste.
4. Place 6 taquitos in air fryer basket (4 on bottom layer, 2 stacked crosswise on top). Cook at 390°F for 8 minutes, until crispy and brown.
5. Repeat step 4 to cook remaining taquitos.
6. Serve plain or with salsa, sour cream, or guacamole for dipping.

Cheese Ravioli

Ingredients:

- 1 egg
- ¼ C. milk
- 1 C. breadcrumbs
- 2 tsp. Italian seasoning
- ⅛ tsp. ground rosemary
- ¼ tsp. basil
- ¼ tsp. parsley
- 9-ounce package uncooked cheese ravioli
- ¼ C. flour
- oil for misting or cooking spray

Servings: 4
Cooking Time:
9 Mins.

Directions:

1. Preheat air fryer to 390°F.
2. In a medium bowl, beat together egg and milk.
3. In a large plastic bag, mix together the breadcrumbs, Italian seasoning, rosemary, basil, and parsley.
4. Place all the ravioli and the flour in a bag or a bowl with a lid and shake to coat.
5. Working with a handful at a time, drop floured ravioli into egg wash. Remove ravioli, letting excess drip off, and place in bag with breadcrumbs.
6. When all ravioli are in the breadcrumbs' bag, shake well to coat all pieces.
7. Dump enough ravioli into air fryer basket to form one layer. Mist with oil or cooking spray. Dump the remaining ravioli on top of the first layer and mist with oil.
8. Cook for 5minutes. Shake well and spray with oil. Break apart any ravioli stuck together and spray any spots you missed the first time.
9. Cook 4 Mins. longer, until ravioli puff up and are crispy golden brown.

Falafel

Ingredients:

- 1 C. dried chickpeas
- ½ onion, chopped
- 1 clove garlic
- ¼ C. fresh parsley leaves
- 1 tsp. salt
- ¼ tsp. crushed red pepper flakes
- 1 tsp. ground cumin
- ½ tsp. ground coriander
- 1 to 2 tbsp. flour
- olive oil
- Tomato Salad
- 2 tomatoes, seeds removed and diced
- ½ cucumber, finely diced
- ¼ red onion, finely diced and rinsed with water
- 1 tsp. red wine vinegar
- 1 tbsp. olive oil
- salt and freshly ground black pepper
- 2 tbsp. chopped fresh parsley

Servings: 4
Cooking Time:
10 Mins.

Directions:

1. Cover the chickpeas with water and let them soak overnight on the counter. Then drain the chickpeas and put them in a food processor, along with the onion, garlic, parsley, spices and 1 tbsp. of flour. Pulse in the food processor until the mixture has broken down into a coarse paste consistency. The mixture should hold together when you pinch it. Add more flour as needed, until you get this consistency.
2. Scoop portions of the mixture (about 2 tbsp. in size) and shape into balls. Place the balls on a plate and refrigerate for at least 30 minutes. You should have between 12 and 14 balls.
3. Preheat the air fryer to 380°F.
4. Spray the falafel balls with oil and place them in the air fryer. Air-fry for 10 minutes, rolling them over and spraying them with oil again halfway through the cooking time so that they cook and brown evenly.
5. Serve with pita bread, hummus, cucumbers, hot peppers, tomatoes or any other fillings you might like.

Roasted Vegetable, Brown Rice And Black Bean Burrito

Ingredients:

- ½ zucchini, sliced ¼-inch thick
- ½ red onion, sliced
- 1 yellow bell pepper, sliced
- 2 tsp. olive oil
- salt and freshly ground black pepper
- 2 burrito size flour tortillas
- 1 C. grated pepper jack cheese
- ½ C. cooked brown rice
- ½ C. canned black beans, drained and rinsed
- ¼ tsp. ground cumin
- 1 tbsp. chopped fresh cilantro
- fresh salsa, guacamole and sour cream, for serving

Directions:

1. Preheat the air fryer to 400°F.
2. Toss the vegetables in a bowl with the olive oil, salt and freshly ground black pepper. Air-fry at 400°F for 12 to 15 minutes, shaking the basket a few times during the cooking process. The vegetables are done when they are cooked to your liking.
3. In the meantime, start building the burritos. Lay the tortillas out on the counter. Sprinkle half of the cheese in the center of the tortillas. Combine the rice, beans, cumin and cilantro in a bowl, season to taste with salt and freshly ground black pepper and then divide the mixture between the two tortillas. When the vegetables have finished cooking, transfer them to the two tortillas, placing the vegetables on top of the rice and beans. Sprinkle the remaining cheese on top and then roll the burritos up, tucking in the sides of the tortillas as you roll. Brush or spray the outside of the burritos with olive oil and transfer them to the air fryer.
4. Air-fry at 360°F for 8 minutes, turning them over when there are about 2 Mins. left. The burritos will have slightly brown spots, but will still be pliable.
5. Serve with some fresh salsa, guacamole and sour cream.

Veggie Fried Rice

Ingredients:

- 1 C. cooked brown rice
- ⅓ C. chopped onion
- ½ C. chopped carrots
- ½ C. chopped bell peppers
- ½ C. chopped broccoli florets
- 3 tbsp. low-sodium soy sauce
- 1 tbsp. sesame oil
- 1 tsp. ground ginger
- 1 tsp. ground garlic powder
- ½ tsp. black pepper
- ⅛ tsp. salt
- 2 large eggs

**Servings: 4
Cooking Time:
25 Mins.**

Directions:

1. Preheat the air fryer to 370°F.
2. In a large bowl, mix together the brown rice, onions, carrots, bell pepper, and broccoli.
3. In a small bowl, whisk together the soy sauce, sesame oil, ginger, garlic powder, pepper, salt, and eggs.
4. Pour the egg mixture into the rice and vegetable mixture and mix together.
5. Liberally spray a 7-inch springform pan (or compatible air fryer dish) with olive oil. Add the rice mixture to the pan and cover with aluminum foil.
6. Place a metal trivet into the air fryer basket and set the pan on top. Cook for 15 minutes. Carefully remove the pan from basket, discard the foil, and mix the rice. Return the rice to the air fryer basket, turning down the temperature to 350°F and cooking another 10 minutes.
7. Remove and let cool 5 minutes. Serve warm.

Tandoori Paneer Naan Pizza

Ingredients:

- 6 tbsp. plain Greek yogurt, divided
- 1¼ tsp. garam marsala, divided
- ½ tsp. turmeric, divided
- ¼ tsp. garlic powder
- ½ tsp. paprika, divided
- ½ tsp. black pepper, divided
- 3 oz. paneer, cut into small cubes
- 1 tbsp. extra-virgin olive oil
- 2 tsp. minced garlic
- 4 C. baby spinach
- 2 tbsp. marinara sauce
- ¼ tsp. salt
- 2 plain naan breads (approximately 6 inches in diameter)
- ½ C. shredded part-skim mozzarella cheese

Servings: 4
Cooking Time: 10 Mins.

Directions:

1. Preheat the air fryer to 350°F.
2. In a small bowl, mix 2 tbsp. of the yogurt, ½ tsp. of the garam marsala, ¼ tsp. of the turmeric, the garlic powder, ¼ tsp. of the paprika, and ¼ tsp. of the black pepper. Toss the paneer cubes in the mixture and let marinate for at least an hour.
3. Meanwhile, in a pan, heat the olive oil over medium heat. Add in the minced garlic and sauté for 1 minute. Stir in the spinach and begin to cook until it wilts. Add in the remaining 4 tbsp. of yogurt and the marinara sauce. Stir in the remaining ¾ tsp. of garam masala, the remaining ¼ tsp. of turmeric, the remaining ¼ tsp. of paprika, the remaining ¼ tsp. of black pepper, and the salt. Let simmer a minute or two, and then remove from the heat.
4. Equally divide the spinach mixture amongst the two naan breads. Place 1½ oz. of the marinated paneer on each naan.
5. Liberally spray the air fryer basket with olive oil mist.
6. Use a spatula to pick up one naan and place it in the air fryer basket.
7. Cook for 4 minutes, open the basket and sprinkle ¼ C. of mozzarella cheese on top, and cook another 4 minutes.
8. Remove from the air fryer and repeat with the remaining naan.
9. Serve warm.

Asparagus, Mushroom And Cheese Soufflés

Ingredients:

Servings: 3
Cooking Time:
21 Mins.

- butter
- grated Parmesan cheese
- 3 button mushrooms, thinly sliced
- 8 spears asparagus, sliced ½-inch long
- 1 tsp. olive oil
- 1 tbsp. butter
- 4½ tsp. flour
- pinch paprika
- pinch ground nutmeg
- salt and freshly ground black pepper
- ½ C. milk
- ½ C. grated Gruyère cheese or other Swiss cheese (about 2 ounces)
- 2 eggs, separated

Directions:

1. Butter three 6-ounce ramekins and dust with grated Parmesan cheese. (Butter the ramekins and then coat the butter with Parmesan by shaking it around in the ramekin and dumping out any excess.)

2. Preheat the air fryer to 400°F.

3. Toss the mushrooms and asparagus in a bowl with the olive oil. Transfer the vegetables to the air fryer and air-fry for 7 minutes, shaking the basket once or twice to redistribute the Ingredients while they cook.

4. While the vegetables are cooking, make the soufflé base. Melt the butter in a saucepan on the stovetop over medium heat. Add the flour, stir and cook for a minute or two. Add the paprika, nutmeg, salt and pepper. Whisk in the milk and bring the mixture to a simmer to thicken. Remove the pan from the heat and add the cheese, stirring to melt. Let the mixture cool for just a few Mins. and then whisk the egg yolks in, one at a time. Stir in the cooked mushrooms and asparagus. Let this soufflé base cool.

5. In a separate bowl, whisk the egg whites to soft peak stage (the point at which the whites can almost stand up on the end of your whisk). Fold the whipped egg whites into the soufflé base, adding a little at a time.

6. Preheat the air fryer to 330°F.

7. Transfer the batter carefully to the buttered ramekins, leaving about ½-inch at the top. Place the ramekins into the air fryer basket and air-fry for 14 minutes. The soufflés should have risen nicely and be brown on top. Serve immediately.

VEGETABLE SIDE DISHES RECIPES

Parmesan Asparagus

Ingredients:

- 1 bunch asparagus, stems trimmed
- 1 tsp. olive oil
- salt and freshly ground black pepper
- ¼ C. coarsely grated Parmesan cheese
- ½ lemon

Servings: 2
Cooking Time:
5 Mins.

Directions:

1. Preheat the air fryer to 400°F.
2. Toss the asparagus with the oil and season with salt and freshly ground black pepper.
3. Transfer the asparagus to the air fryer basket and air-fry at 400°F for 5 minutes, shaking the basket to turn the asparagus once or twice during the cooking process.
4. When the asparagus is cooked to your liking, sprinkle the asparagus generously with the Parmesan cheese and close the air fryer drawer again. Let the asparagus sit for 1 minute in the turned-off air fryer. Then, remove the asparagus, transfer it to a serving dish and finish with a grind of black pepper and a squeeze of lemon juice.

Rosemary Roasted Potatoes With Lemon

Ingredients:

- 1 lb. small red-skinned potatoes, halved or cut into bite-sized chunks
- 1 tbsp. olive oil
- 1 tsp. finely chopped fresh rosemary
- ¼ tsp. salt
- freshly ground black pepper
- 1 tbsp. lemon zest

Servings: 4
Cooking Time:
12 Mins.

Directions:

1. Preheat the air fryer to 400°F.
2. Toss the potatoes with the olive oil, rosemary, salt and freshly ground black pepper.
3. Air-fry for 12 Mins. (depending on the size of the chunks), tossing the potatoes a few times throughout the cooking process.
4. As soon as the potatoes are tender to a knifepoint, toss them with the lemon zest and more salt if desired.

Curried Cauliflower With Cashews And Yogurt

Ingredients:

Servings: 2
Cooking Time: 12 Mins.

- 4 C. cauliflower florets (about half a large head)
- 1 tbsp. olive oil
- salt
- 1 tsp. curry powder
- ½ C. toasted, chopped cashews
- Cool Yogurt Drizzle
- ¼ C. plain yogurt
- 2 tbsp. sour cream
- 1 tsp. lemon juice
- pinch cayenne pepper
- salt
- 1 tsp. honey
- 1 tbsp. chopped fresh cilantro, plus leaves for garnish

Directions:

1. Preheat the air fryer to 400°F.
2. Toss the cauliflower florets with the olive oil, salt and curry powder, coating evenly.
3. Transfer the cauliflower to the air fryer basket and air-fry at 400°F for 12 minutes, shaking the basket a couple of times during the cooking process.
4. While the cauliflower is cooking, make the cool yogurt drizzle by combining all ingredients in a bowl.
5. When the cauliflower is cooked to your liking, serve it warm with the cool yogurt either underneath or drizzled over the top. Scatter the cashews and cilantro leaves around.

Bacon-wrapped Asparagus

Ingredients:

- 1 tbsp. extra-virgin olive oil
- ½ tsp. sea salt
- ¼ C. grated Parmesan cheese
- 1 lb. asparagus, ends trimmed
- 8 slices bacon

Servings: 4
Cooking Time:
10 Mins.

Directions:

1. Preheat the air fryer to 380°F.
2. In large bowl, mix together the olive oil, sea salt, and Parmesan cheese. Toss the asparagus in the olive oil mixture.
3. Evenly divide the asparagus into 8 bundles. Wrap 1 piece of bacon around each bundle, not overlapping the bacon but spreading it across the bundle.
4. Place the asparagus bundles into the air fryer basket, not touching. Work in batches as needed.
5. Cook for 8 minutes; check for doneness, and cook another 2 minutes.

Sweet Potato Fries

Ingredients:

- 2 lb. sweet potatoes
- 1 tsp. dried marjoram
- 2 tsp. olive oil
- sea salt

Servings: 4
Cooking Time:
30 Mins.

Directions:

1. Peel and cut the potatoes into ¼-inch sticks, 4 to 5 inches long.
2. In a sealable plastic bag or bowl with lid, toss sweet potatoes with marjoram and olive oil. Rub seasonings in to coat well.
3. Pour sweet potatoes into air fryer basket and cook at 390°F for approximately 30 minutes, until cooked through with some brown spots on edges.
4. Season to taste with sea salt.

Chicken Eggrolls

Ingredients:

- 1 tbsp. vegetable oil
- ¼ C. chopped onion
- 1 clove garlic, minced
- 1 C. shredded carrot
- ½ C. thinly sliced celery
- 2 C. cooked chicken
- 2 C. shredded white cabbage
- ½ C. teriyaki sauce
- 20 egg roll wrappers
- 1 egg, whisked
- 1 tbsp. water

Directions:

1. Preheat the air fryer to 390°F.
2. In a large skillet, heat the oil over medium-high heat. Add in the onion and sauté for 1 minute. Add in the garlic and sauté for 30 seconds. Add in the carrot and celery and cook for 2 minutes. Add in the chicken, cabbage, and teriyaki sauce. Allow the mixture to cook for 1 minute, stirring to combine. Remove from the heat.
3. In a small bowl, whisk together the egg and water for brushing the edges.
4. Lay the eggroll wrappers out at an angle. Place ¼ C. filling in the center. Fold the bottom corner up first and then fold in the corners; roll up to complete eggroll.
5. Place the eggrolls in the air fryer basket, spray with cooking spray, and cook for 8 minutes, turn over, and cook another 2 to 4 minutes.

Roasted Yellow Squash And Onions

Ingredients:

Servings: 3
Cooking Time:
20 Mins.

- 1 medium (8-inch) squash Yellow or summer crookneck squash, cut into ½-inch-thick rounds
- 1½ C. (1 large onion) Yellow or white onion, roughly chopped
- ¾ tsp. Table salt
- ¼ tsp. Ground cumin (optional)
- Olive oil spray
- 1½ tbsp. Lemon or lime juice

Directions:

1. Preheat the air fryer to 375°F .

2. Toss the squash rounds, onion, salt, and cumin (if using) in a large bowl. Lightly coat the vegetables with olive oil spray, toss again, spray again, and keep at it until the vegetables are evenly coated.

3. When the machine is at temperature, scrape the contents of the bowl into the basket, spreading the vegetables out into as close to one layer as you can. Air-fry for 20 minutes, tossing once very gently, until the squash and onions are soft, even a little browned at the edges.

4. Pour the contents of the basket into a serving bowl, add the lemon or lime juice, and toss gently but well to coat. Serve warm or at room temperature.

Smashed Fried Baby Potatoes

Ingredients:

- 1½ lb. baby red or baby Yukon gold potatoes
- ¼ C. butter, melted
- 1 tsp. olive oil
- ½ tsp. paprika
- 1 tsp. dried parsley
- salt and freshly ground black pepper
- 2 scallions, finely chopped

Servings: 3
Cooking Time:
18 Mins.

Directions:

1. Bring a large pot of salted water to a boil. Add the potatoes and boil for 18 Mins. or until the potatoes are fork-tender.

2. Drain the potatoes and transfer them to a cutting board to cool slightly. Spray or brush the bottom of a drinking glass with a little oil. Smash or flatten the potatoes by pressing the glass down on each potato slowly. Try not to completely flatten the potato or smash it so hard that it breaks apart.

3. Combine the melted butter, olive oil, paprika, and parsley together.

4. Preheat the air fryer to 400°F.

5. Spray the bottom of the air fryer basket with oil and transfer one layer of the smashed potatoes into the basket. Brush with some of the butter mixture and season generously with salt and freshly ground black pepper.

6. Air-fry at 400°F for 10 minutes. Carefully flip the potatoes over and air-fry for an additional 8 Mins. until crispy and lightly browned.

7. Keep the potatoes warm in a 170°F oven or tent with aluminum foil while you cook the second batch. Sprinkle minced scallions over the potatoes and serve warm.

Printed in Great Britain
by Amazon

87152982R00054